CW00344967

Disposing of the Body

Other playtexts recently published by Amber Lane Press include

SAMUEL ADAMSON

Clocks and Whistles
Grace Note

CARLO ARDITO

Brief Candle and Other Plays

'BIYI BANDELE

Death Catches the Hunter
Marching for Fausa
Resurrections
Two Horsemen
Oroonoko (adapted from Aphra Behn)

JULIAN MITCHELL

August
Falling Over England

ALAN PLATER

I Thought I Heard a Rustling

MARTIN SHERMAN

A Madhouse in Goa
Some Sunny Day

KUNIO SHIMIZU

Tango at the End of Winter

AUGUST STRINDBERG

The Father; Lady Julie; Playing with Fire
Motherly Love; Pariah; The First Warning

HUGH WHITEMORE

A Letter of Resignation
It's Ralph

For a free copy of our complete list of plays and theatre books write to:
Amber Lane Press, Church Street, Charlbury, Oxon OX7 3PR
Telephone and fax: 01608 810024

Hugh Whitemore

Disposing of
the Body

AMBER LANE PRESS

All rights whatsoever in this play are strictly reserved and application for professional performance should be made before rehearsals begin to:
Judy Daish Associates Ltd,
2 St Charles Place,
London W10 6EG

Application for amateur performance should be made before rehearsals begin to:
Samuel French Ltd,
52 Fitzroy Street,
London W1P 6JR

No performance may be given unless a licence has been obtained.

First published in 1999 by
Amber Lane Press Ltd,
Church Street, Charlbury, Oxford OX7 3PR
Telephone: 01608 810024

Printed and bound by
The Guernsey Press Co Ltd, Guernsey, C.I.

Copyright © Hugh Whitemore, 1999
The right of HUGH WHITEMORE to be identified as author of this Work has been asserted by him in accordance with the Copyright, Designs and Patents Act, 1988

ISBN 1 872868 27 4

CONDITIONS OF SALE
This book is sold subject to the condition that it shall not, by way of trade or otherwise, be lent, re-sold, hired out or otherwise circulated without the publisher's prior consent in any form of binding or cover other than that in which it is published and without a similar condition, including this condition being imposed on the subsequent purchaser.

CHARACTERS

HENRY PREECE

ANGELA, his wife

BEN, their son

ALEXANDER BARLEY

JOANNA, his wife

KATE PREECE, Henry's sister

DETECTIVE-INSPECTOR CLIVE POOLE

BASSETT, a hotel manager

The action takes place in England:
partly in London, but mostly in the country

Time: the present

Disposing of the Body was first presented at the Hampstead Theatre, London, on 13th July 1999, with the following cast:

HENRY . . . Stephen Moore
ANGELA . . . Charlotte Cornwell
BEN . . . Ben Porter
ALEXANDER . . . David Horovitch
JOANNA . . . Gemma Jones
KATE . . . Joanna McCallum
INSPECTOR POOLE . . . Ken Drury
BASSETT . . . James Benson

Director: Robin Lefèvre
Designer: Tom Piper
Lighting: Mick Hughes
Composer/Sound Design: Anders Sodergren

ACT ONE

The set should suggest various English interiors: screens, perhaps, or panels, some of which can be opened to reveal trees. Furniture should be kept to a minimum.

London. Spring. Afternoon.

HENRY PREECE *is wrapping cups and saucers in newspaper and stacking them in a tea-chest. A second, full, tea-chest stands nearby.* HENRY *is in his fifties: reassuringly conventional in appearance and manner.* ANGELA, *his wife, enters: pert and pretty, late forties, wearing outdoor clothes.*

ANGELA What are you doing?

HENRY Almost finished.

ANGELA You shouldn't be doing that.

HENRY Why not?

ANGELA The men like to do it themselves —

HENRY I thought it might save a bit of time.

ANGELA — in case something gets broken. It affects the insurance if you do it.

HENRY Oh well, never mind.

[*He continues wrapping and stacking.*]

The bank telephoned. The financial stuff happens tomorrow. It's all done by computer. Nobody even writes a cheque. You'd think they'd give you something.

[ANGELA *is removing her coat.*]

ANGELA Give you what?

HENRY A piece of paper. Some sort of notification. Huge sums of money change hands, and it's just a blip on a computer screen. [*He wraps and stacks the last cup.*] What was the name of the man who sold us this house?

ANGELA Harris.

HENRY   Harris. Of course. I've been trying to remember all af-
        ternoon.

ANGELA Why?

HENRY   I was thinking about the day we came to measure up
        for the curtains — do you remember? Mr Harris and
        I were standing by the bedroom window. 'Look at that
        tree,' he said. 'There's a knobbly bit where the two
        big branches join. It's like a face.' And as I looked, I
        could see it. A funny pointed nose, bulging eyes and
        a smile. I've never seen it again. I've looked out of that
        window hundreds of times, thousands of times, and
        I've never seen that face again. Why is that? And now
        I never shall.

ANGELA Why are you sad?

HENRY   I'm not sad.

ANGELA You seem sad.

HENRY   Tired.

ANGELA It's been a long day.

HENRY   I hope we're doing the right thing.

ANGELA You know we are.

HENRY   We were young when we came here. A young
        couple with a baby. When we get to Stoke Amberley
        people will think of us as middle-aged. Which we are,
        of course. A middle-aged couple with a grown-up son.

ANGELA What's wrong with that?

HENRY   Nothing.

              [*He embraces her.*]

        Pay no attention. I'm tired. All is well.

              [HENRY *exits. The tea-chests are removed.*]

ANGELA We didn't choose Gloucestershire, it was one of those
        things, fate, or whatever. Henry's sister lives near
        Tetbury and we were going there for lunch. We were

early, so we stopped in Cirencester and had a look at the shops. On a sudden impulse we went into an estate agent's and put our names on his list. Three weeks later he sent us details of the cottage at Stoke Amberley.

Early summer. Trees. Evening.

ANGELA Half a mile from the village. Not another house in sight. A few days after we moved in our nearest neighbours — Joanna and Alexander Barley — rang up and asked us round for a drink.

> [HENRY *enters with* JOANNA *and* ALEXANDER BARLEY. *They are in their middle forties.* ALEXANDER *is heavily built, with a confident, hearty manner;* JOANNA *is pleasant but plain. They are both wearing comfortable country clothes.*]

ALEXANDER I take no credit for the garden. It's all thanks to Jo.

HENRY Very nice. Lovely trees.

ANGELA Ours is more like a jungle.

JOANNA So was this when we moved in.

HENRY It's a bit uncared-for, that's all.

ANGELA 'Delightful rambling garden,' it said in the estate agent's blurb. We should've complained.

HENRY I rather like it.

ANGELA They might've knocked something off the price.

JOANNA We got an amazing thing to get rid of the undergrowth — what's it called? — the fire thing.

ALEXANDER A flame-gun.

JOANNA Yes, a flame-gun. It burns up all the weeds and undergrowth. It's marvellous.

ALEXANDER Yes, you'll need a flame-gun — and a rotovator. Go to the hire shop in Cirencester.

JOANNA Are you gardeners?

ANGELA Henry is. We had quite a big garden in London.

HENRY Not big.

ANGELA Big by London standards.

HENRY Biggish.

ANGELA How much land have you got?

JOANNA Almost an acre. Right down to the river.

ANGELA I didn't know there was a river.

ALEXANDER There's not. Jo calls it a river. In actual fact it's a piddling little stream, scarcely more than a ditch.

JOANNA That's not true. It's on maps. It's got a name.

ALEXANDER She thinks it's romantic to have a river at the bottom of the garden.

ANGELA So it is.

JOANNA It's on the Ordnance Survey map. It's called the River Stoat.

ALEXANDER As in weasel.

JOANNA Come and see.

ANGELA Yes, I'd like to.

ALEXANDER What about a drink? Or is it too early?

HENRY Not too early for me.

ALEXANDER I suppose we should have champagne to welcome you to Stoke Amberley — all we have is a modest muscadet.

HENRY Very nice.

ALEXANDER Angela?

ANGELA Let's have a look at the river first.

JOANNA You don't have to.

ANGELA I'd like to.

ALEXANDER Be careful not to fall in. You might get your feet wet.

[ALEXANDER *laughs*. ANGELA *and* JOANNA *exit*. ALEXANDER *fetches wine, glasses and a bowl of nuts.*]

ALEXANDER So. What brought you to this part of the world?

HENRY Nothing in particular. Kate, my sister, lives near Tetbury, so we knew the area slightly.

ALEXANDER Well anything's better than London. So smelly. Don't you find that?

HENRY I suppose I'm used to it.

ALEXANDER Paris smells of chestnuts and Gauloises. London smells of urine. Cheers.

HENRY Cheers.

ALEXANDER Do you have any children?

HENRY A son. Ben. He's in America, doing medical research. What about you?

ALEXANDER Two. Both married. Daughters. Have a nut.

HENRY Thanks.

ALEXANDER Jo says you're taking early retirement.

HENRY I was fired. Made redundant, as they say.

ALEXANDER Dear-oh-dear.

HENRY It's not as bad as it sounds. Financially there's no problem — but I miss the routine. It seems very odd, getting up in the morning with nothing to do and nowhere to go.

ALEXANDER Sounds pretty damn good to me.

HENRY What do you do?

ALEXANDER Guess.

[HENRY *gives him a long look.*]

HENRY Schoolmaster.

ALEXANDER Jo told you.

HENRY No.

ALEXANDER All right — what do I teach?

[*Another long look.*]

HENRY Languages.

ALEXANDER Which one?

HENRY   German.

ALEXANDER   French. I do wish I wasn't so easily pigeon-holed.

HENRY   You're not. Lucky guess.

ALEXANDER   No, no, it happens all the time. There was a Parents' Evening last week. I strolled in, looking, as I thought, totally anonymous. Whereupon a vigorous and bossy woman came up to me and said, 'You must be Alexander Barley, I'd recognise you anywhere.' What do you suppose she meant by that? I felt as if I'd got a label tied around my neck like Paddington Bear.

HENRY   I do like your name.

ALEXANDER   Alexander?

HENRY   Barley.

ALEXANDER   Old English, found chiefly in Lancashire and Cheshire. Yours, of course, is Welsh. A contraction of Ap-Rhys. Ap being Welsh for son of. Ap-Rhys. Son of Rhys. Preece. [*grins*] I'm full of useless snippets of information. One of my schoolmasterly failings.

[ANGELA *and* JOANNA *enter.*]

JOANNA   What is?

ALEXANDER   Picking my nose. How was the river?

ANGELA   Enchanting. You must go and see it, Henry.

ALEXANDER   Glass of wine?

ANGELA   Please. Jo's looking for a job.

HENRY   Oh really?

ANGELA   Something part-time. Secretarial. Just right for you.

ALEXANDER   If you want a secretary, Jo's your girl. Fantastic. Eighty words a minute.

JOANNA   Not now. I used to be.

HENRY   Well, it's early days. I'm not sure what I want at the moment.

ANGELA   You need someone *now*, Henry.

HENRY   Do I?

ANGELA You know you do. He's hopeless at organising things.

ALEXANDER Have a nut.

> [*Lights fade on* ALEXANDER, JOANNA *and* ANGELA.]

HENRY We finished off the bottle of wine and got home about half-past seven. Angela went to the kitchen to prepare supper. I could hear her clattering about with plates and saucepans. For a fastidious woman she's surprisingly clumsy. I went upstairs to the room I had rather pretentiously christened my study. I sat on the sofa. It was a beautiful evening. I felt unexpectedly happy. I felt sure that if a passing stranger were to look in at the lighted windows of my house, he would say to himself, 'There lives a lucky man.'

> [ANGELA *goes to* HENRY.]

ANGELA Supper in half an hour.

HENRY Fine.

ANGELA They seem very pleasant.

HENRY Don't they.

ANGELA You must talk to her about work.

HENRY Must I?

ANGELA Don't you like her?

HENRY She's all right. A bit fey.

ANGELA Fey?

HENRY All that stuff about the river.

ANGELA What's fey about that? You'll have to get someone to help you. Why not her?

HENRY Let me think about it.

ANGELA She used to work part-time for an architect in Cirencester. He went bust last year. She's looking for another job.

HENRY I couldn't pay her much.

ANGELA She wouldn't expect you to.

> [ANGELA *and* HENRY *exit.*]

Morning. JOANNA *enters.*

JOANNA   Henry rang the following week. 'Come and have a cup of coffee,' he said. I was feeling tired. I had my period. I nearly didn't go.

[HENRY *enters with a coffee tray.*]

HENRY   You'd probably find it very boring. Basically it's just typing.

JOANNA   Typing what?

HENRY   Well, I — black or white?

JOANNA   White, please.

HENRY   I've got this project, you see... [*pours the milk*] Old gramophone records. Sugar?

JOANNA   No, thanks.

[HENRY *gives a cup to* JOANNA.]

Thank you. Old gramophone records?

HENRY   It all started years ago. When I was a boy. [*sits and sips his coffee*] For most of my working life I was with a company that makes loudspeakers. High quality; top end of the market. The company was started by a friend of mine. Graham. Graham Walker. My first job was with the BBC, on the technical side, so I knew something about audio-electronics. Graham and I became partners in 1968 — and we did very well. But, as I say, we always concentrated on the top end of the market. Nothing but the best: that was Graham's motto. Now, of course, things have got to change.

JOANNA   Why is that?

HENRY   Ah, well — everything changes. The recession didn't help. Then Graham became ill. His son took over the business. Hence the reorganisation. Hence my departure.

JOANNA   How rotten for you.

HENRY   These things happen. Biscuit?

JOANNA Thanks.

HENRY Anyway, I've always collected gramophone records, ever since I was a boy — so did my father. He had hundreds of them — old 78s — all stacked away neatly in brown paper sleeves. He didn't have very exalted taste in music, my old dad — middle-of-the-road stuff, mostly — light orchestral, operetta, popular classics. A lot of these records were HMV records, and they had a distinctive plum-coloured label. Collectors called them plum label records. Well, I became fascinated by them. Not just because of the music, but because of the way of life they seemed to represent: the lower-middle-class world of the thirties and forties — privet hedges, fumed oak furniture, *Children's Hour* on the radio. I had the idea of compiling an annotated catalogue of all plum label records. Then I thought perhaps I could make it into some sort of social history, using the plum label as a symbol for the world I grew up in. So there we are: that's what it's all about.

JOANNA I think that's a really good idea.

HENRY You don't have to say that.

JOANNA I mean it. It sounds fascinating.

HENRY Well, it fascinates me.

JOANNA What exactly would you want me to do?

HENRY As I say — typing. Mostly. Sorting out the research stuff I've already done and then typing it up.

JOANNA Fine.

HENRY Would that be all right?

JOANNA Absolutely. How many hours would you need me?

HENRY Hard to say. Two afternoons a week?

JOANNA Fine.

HENRY What about money?

> [*She turns from him.*]

JOANNA   Suddenly I felt sad. I could imagine how it must've been when they started the business. Henry and his friend, Graham. Two young men, so keen to succeed. 'Nothing but the best.' And now everything's changed. Money was discussed with the usual English embarrassment. We settled for eight pounds an hour. Tuesdays and Thursdays.

HENRY   She came at half-past one and left at half-past five. Punctual to the minute.

JOANNA   He made me laugh a lot. I wasn't expecting that.

> [JOANNA *exits.*]

> [HENRY *goes to the telephone and dials a number.* BEN *enters: late twenties, tall, strongly built, bearded.*]

BEN   Hi, this is Ben Preece. Sorry I can't take your call at the moment. If it's urgent you could try the clinic — area code 310, 832 4646 — otherwise leave a message after the beep. Thanks.

> [HENRY *hangs up.* BEN *exits.*]

> [ANGELA *enters.*]

HENRY   Ben's out.

ANGELA   What?

HENRY   I just rang Ben. He's not there.

ANGELA   Probably at work.

HENRY   It's breakfast time in L.A. Isn't it? Eight hours back.

ANGELA   Try again later.

HENRY   I wonder what his life is. We know nothing about it, not a thing.

ANGELA   We wouldn't know much more if he lived in London.

HENRY   Wouldn't we? No, I suppose not.

ANGELA   Is Kate still on that funny diet?

HENRY   I'm not sure.

ANGELA   I thought I'd give her lamb for dinner, would that be all right?

HENRY   Oh yes, she likes lamb.

ANGELA   Gazpacho, lamb and summer pudding.

HENRY   Perfect.

ANGELA   Shall we ask Alexander and Jo?

HENRY   If you like.

ANGELA   Why don't you ring them? Say next Tuesday, seven-thirty for eight.

> [ANGELA *exits.*]
>
> [HENRY *dials a number.* BEN *enters.*]

BEN   Hi, this is Ben Preece. Sorry I can't take your call at the moment. If it's urgent you could try the clinic — area code 310, 832 4646 — otherwise leave a message after the beep. Thanks.

HENRY   Ben, it's Dad. How are you? Nothing much to say, really. No news of any import. Just wondered how you are. Seems a long time since we spoke.

How's life? Are you busy? How's Santa Monica?

We miss you, Ben. We miss you being here. I've never really appreciated the happy times of my life until they were over and out of reach. Avoid that mistake if you can. Sorry, I'm getting sentimental. Something to do with living in the country. More time to think.

What a ridiculous message this is. Why can't I erase it? Why can't technology handle that? Ring us when you can. Much love. 'Bye.

> [HENRY *hangs up.* BEN *exits.*]

A warm evening. Garden terrace. ALEXANDER *and* JOANNA *enter with* KATE, HENRY's *sister. She is in her late forties: big, jolly, comfortable.* HENRY *pours wine.*

ALEXANDER   Sorry, I'm confused. I thought Henry said you lived in Cirencester.

KATE   Tetbury.

HENRY   We were on our way to lunch with Kate — we were early — so we stopped at Cirencester.

ALEXANDER   Tetbury via Cirencester...?

HENRY   I can't bear the M4.

KATE   Henry goes to enormous lengths to avoid driving on the motorway.

ALEXANDER   Do you?

JOANNA   So if you'd gone on the M4 and hadn't been early for lunch, you wouldn't have gone to the estate agents.

HENRY   I suppose not.

JOANNA   You wouldn't have bought this house, we wouldn't have met, and we wouldn't be here tonight. We'd all be somewhere else, doing something completely different.

ALEXANDER   What are you saying?

JOANNA   Well, nothing.

ALEXANDER   Jo likes to find significance in trivial events. I think she finds it comforting.

JOANNA   No I don't. I just find it curious, the way things happen.

ALEXANDER   Yes, but you're implying there's some sort of mysterious thread linking it all together.

HENRY   Perhaps there is.

ALEXANDER   Oho! — a fellow believer.

ANGELA   [*off*] Dinner in five minutes!

[HENRY *and* KATE *exit.*]

ALEXANDER   The wine went straight to my head. Jo kept glaring at me. We had stuffed lamb. The stuffing was so strongly flavoured you couldn't taste anything else. We talked about gardens and overdrafts and holidays abroad. Ten, fifteen years ago we had supper parties not dinner parties. The food was simple and the evenings were full of lively and impassioned argument. Now everybody agrees with everybody else. Is this middle age? Is it a mature understanding of the other person's point of view? Or is it just laziness?

[ALEXANDER *exits*.]

Day. JOANNA *enters with* ANGELA.

JOANNA That was a marvellous meal the other night.

ANGELA Thank you.

JOANNA I'm not much of a cook. Alexander's not really interested in food, so there's no great incentive for me to do anything special. He's got what I call a rugby club appetite: quantity rather than quality.

ANGELA He doesn't strike me as the rugby club type.

JOANNA He used to be. He was very keen when he was young.

ANGELA How did you meet?

JOANNA At school.

ANGELA So you've known each other a long time?

JOANNA At the school where we both worked. He was teaching; I was the headmaster's secretary. Great scandal.

ANGELA Why?

JOANNA Oh well, he was married. Didn't you know that? His wife was very active in the school. People liked her a lot. We had to leave. Well, we didn't *have* to. It seemed a good idea. [*Pause*.] How did you meet Henry?

ANGELA I suppose you'd call it a blind date. A friend of mine had tickets for Wimbledon. Somebody cancelled at the last minute. Henry came in his place.

JOANNA Then what?

ANGELA Nothing for ages. Then I bumped into him one lunchtime, near the office where I worked. He asked me out for dinner. Then it began.

JOANNA Isn't it peculiar? The way lives change. It's like we were saying at your dinner party.

ANGELA What was that?

JOANNA   Oh no, you weren't there, you were in the kitchen. We were saying everything happens by chance. One thing leads to another.

ANGELA   Henry left nothing to chance. He found out where I worked. He waited near my office, lunchtime after lunchtime. He planned it all very carefully.

          [JOANNA *finds this oddly disconcerting; there is a moment of silence before she speaks.*]

JOANNA   How long have you been together?

ANGELA   Twenty-eight years.

JOANNA   You're very good at it, aren't you?

ANGELA   What?

JOANNA   Being a wife. Cooking. Entertaining. I keep thinking I'll do those things when I'm grown up. Isn't that ridiculous? Like getting my legs waxed instead of shaving them.

          [*She laughs. She goes to the desk and sits down.*]

ANGELA   I got tickets for the new Simon Gray play. We often go to the theatre in Bath, it's a lovely old theatre and not too far away. Kate usually comes with us. This time she couldn't, so I asked Joanna. Henry was furious. Well, not furious. Cross. He sulked the whole evening. I couldn't understand why. Perhaps she irritates him.

          [ANGELA *exits.* HENRY *enters and dictates to* JOANNA.]

HENRY   The record number is C–3305. The composer, Handel. The title, 'Where'er You Walk' from the opera *Semele* — S–E–M–E–L–E. The singer is Webster Booth.

JOANNA   Webster?

HENRY   Webster, yes. Webster Booth. He had a wife called Anne Ziegler. They sang duets together. Operetta. Sentimental ballads. 'We'll Gather Lilacs in the Spring Again.' He was rather good looking in a nineteen thirty-ish, upper-class sort of way. I used to imagine him having dinner in the Savoy Grill, not that I had the remotest idea what the Savoy Grill was like.

[JOANNA *laughs.*]

Next is B–9719. Again the composer is Handel. The title, 'Silent Worship' from the opera, *Tolomeo* — T–O–L–O–M–E–O. The singer is Heddle Nash.

JOANNA He has beautiful hands. He leant on the desk, reading the page as I typed it. He has the most beautiful hands.

HENRY Angela's cousin died. The third family funeral in eighteen months. It was the sort of gathering I tend to dread, but because I'm no longer working I couldn't get out of it. We spent four tedious days in Saffron Walden. 'Since you've come all this way, you might as well stay for the weekend,' said Leslie, my brother-in-law. I could think of no reasonable excuse. Leslie is one of those middle-aged men with a fat purple neck and a persistent gurgling cough. Two years younger than me; I can't believe it.

[JOANNA *goes to the table and sits down.*]

When I got back home I found that Joanna had typed almost half of my research notes. I was delighted. As a little gesture of thanks I asked her out to lunch. I half expected her to refuse — but she didn't.

[HENRY *goes to the table and sits with* JOANNA. *A* WAITER *serves.*]

JOANNA How are you getting on with the garden?

HENRY Not very well. I'm not much of a gardener.

JOANNA I thought you said you were.

HENRY Angela said I was. [*sips his wine*] It's curious. Gardening and me. Angela tells everyone I'm a keen gardener. I think she believes it to be true. She certainly wants it to be true. She buys me gardening things for birthdays and Christmas. I think she thinks a proper husband should be keen on gardening.

JOANNA   But you're not ...

HENRY   I love gardens — flowers, trees, specially trees; I love gardens, but I can't stand gardening.

JOANNA   Why haven't you told her?

HENRY   Yes, I should've done. Too late now, of course.

JOANNA   Too late ... ?

HENRY   Don't let's talk about it. More wine?

JOANNA   Please.

[HENRY *pours the wine.*]

We're going away next month.

HENRY   Away?

JOANNA   On holiday. I should've told you.

HENRY   Where are you going?

JOANNA   Cornwall. Alexander has friends in Perranporth. I'm sorry, I should've told you.

HENRY   How long will you be away?

JOANNA   Two weeks.

[*Pause. They eat.*]

I think your book's very interesting.

HENRY   Thank you.

JOANNA   Moving, too. You make it seem such a touching, happy time — the thirties and forties. A sort of paradise lost.

HENRY   Perhaps I've been too sentimental. Do you think I have?

JOANNA   Not sentimental, no. Anyway, it's true what you say. Everything *was* very different then. So comforting and secure.

HENRY   Hardly secure. Hardly comforting. War, poverty, oppression, misery. But I suppose there was a firmer structure to life. God watched over us and we had to behave ourselves. We all knew where we were. We had fewer choices.

JOANNA Is that good?

HENRY Yes, I think it is. If you don't have any choice then you tend to make do with what you've got. The more choice you have, the more discontented you become. Wouldn't you say?

JOANNA Perhaps.

HENRY My parents lived in the same house for almost fifty years. My father had the same job; my mother cooked three meals a day and always made the bed before breakfast. They stood up when the National Anthem was played, had fish on Friday, and paid all bills within twenty-four hours of receiving them. I don't think it ever occurred to them to do anything different. Or perhaps it did, I don't know. Anyway, they behaved as if the choice didn't exist — and were probably much happier as a result. Less troubled, certainly.

[*Pause. They eat.*]

JOANNA I dreamt about them the other night. Your parents. We were all in the kitchen. 'Hello,' I said, 'you must be Henry's parents.' They were very kind and help-ful. I was looking for my passport. I think I was going to New York.

HENRY How did you know they were my parents?

JOANNA I just did.

HENRY I don't dream. Hardly ever.

JOANNA You do actually, everybody does, you just don't re-member your dreams. You should train yourself to remember them.

HENRY How do you do that?

JOANNA By telling yourself to remember your dreams just before you go to sleep. Try it. Dreams are very im-portant. [*takes a sip of wine*] It's funny. Me dreaming of your parents. I dream of my father a lot. Perhaps there's some connection.

HENRY Why should there be?

JOANNA There often is in dreams. Hidden connections, hidden meanings. That's why they're important. We can learn from them.

HENRY Is your father still alive?

JOANNA No, he died five years ago. I dream that he walks into the house and I embrace him. 'I thought you were dead,' I say. And he holds me. I wake up with tears in my eyes. I have the same dream three or four times a month. I feel guilty, you see. The dream is about forgiveness. I want him to forgive me.

HENRY For what?

[JOANNA *hesitates.*]

Tell me.

[JOANNA *takes a sip of wine.*]

JOANNA He loved Eastbourne. We used to go there when I was a child. We'd sit on the beach and look at the sea. Have lunch in one of those fusty old-fashioned hotels. Then we'd walk up to Beachy Head. He loved it. When he was ill and dying he wanted to go there again. To say goodbye. So we took him, my mother and me. He was dreadfully ill; and I realised that people were staring at him, because he looked so ill. I was embarrassed and ashamed. I hurried him back to the car. I wish I hadn't done that.

[*A tear trickles down her face.*]

Sorry.

[*She dabs her cheek with the table napkin.*]

HENRY I don't suppose he knew how you felt.

JOANNA Oh yes, I think he did. He knew I was ashamed of him.

HENRY All children are ashamed of their parents. It's axiomatic. My son's ashamed of me. No doubt your daughters are of you.

JOANNA They're not my children. Alexander's by his first marriage.

> [JOANNA *exits.*]

Evening.

HENRY Angela had been to London to see the Royal Academy Summer show. She got home about half-past five.

> [ANGELA *enters.*]

ANGELA Have you heard the news?

HENRY What news?

ANGELA The Prime Minister's been shot.

HENRY Good Lord, is he dead?

ANGELA Shot in the leg. Somebody protesting about a new motorway. I thought it might've been you.

> [ANGELA *exits.*]

Night. HENRY *sits at his desk.*

HENRY It was Thursday evening. Angela went out. She'd joined a cookery circle in Cirencester. A recipe a week, presented in rotation by the members of the group. This week it was Vitello Tonnato, prepared by the assistant manager of the National Westminster Bank. I went to my room and wrote a poem — something I must've done before, I suppose, but I can't remember when.

Hoping to outwit mortality
We all like living other lives:
By watching films or reading stories
Or pursuing our romantic drives.

Falling in love means catching glimpses
Of a life we can never share;
By that I mean a past long buried
And all the people hidden there.

Today at lunch you told a story
About your father on the beach;
And as you spoke I seemed to see him —
Your past, for a moment, within my reach.

But then our noisy world reclaimed us
(the waiter offering sour cream and chives),
Leaving just a plaintive yearning
For living other people's lives.

Day. ALEXANDER *enters.* HENRY *stands to greet him.*

ALEXANDER Am I interrupting?

HENRY Not at all.

ALEXANDER I haven't seen you for ages. Is everything all right?

HENRY Yes, fine. Busy.

ALEXANDER So I gather.

HENRY A lot of typing for Joanna.

ALEXANDER She loves it.

HENRY Does she?

ALEXANDER Loves it.

HENRY I'd be lost without her.

ALEXANDER Really?

HENRY Absolutely.

ALEXANDER Good, I'm delighted. It's important for her, having a job. Gives her an identity of her own.

HENRY She doesn't need a job to give her an identity.

ALEXANDER Well, it's difficult for her sometimes.

HENRY What is?

ALEXANDER We've had our problems.

HENRY You and Joanna?

ALEXANDER Like everyone else. *La vie conjugale.* Anyway, I'm grateful.

HENRY For what?

ALEXANDER   The job. It's been a godsend for Jo.

            [*Pause.*]

HENRY   How are things at school?

ALEXANDER   Pretty bloody boring. Does she ever talk about Rebecca?

HENRY   Who's Rebecca?

ALEXANDER   My eldest daughter. I wondered if Jo ever talked about her.

HENRY   No. Why?

ALEXANDER   There was a bit of friction when the marriage bust up. Jo and Rebecca don't see eye to eye. I wondered if she ever mentioned it.

HENRY   No, never.

ALEXANDER   Fine, not to worry.

            [*He gives a piece of paper to* HENRY.]

            Look: this is our phone number in Cornwall. Just in case the house burns down.

HENRY   Right.

            [ALEXANDER *grasps* HENRY *by the arm.*]

ALEXANDER   You're a good chap, Henry.

            [ALEXANDER *exits.*]

HENRY   And so they went on holiday. It was odd without Joanna. We seemed to understand each other. I liked the clothes she wore. We laughed a lot. I pinned their Cornwall number to the notice-board in my study. I looked at it every day. Then suddenly, as if obeying a mysterious command, I found myself dialling the number. A man answered. Mercifully it wasn't Alexander. 'Is that 856532?' I said, deliberately making a mistake. '856533,' he said. I could hear voices in the background. It sounded very jolly. I tried to prolong the conversation. Then I heard Joanna laugh. Unmistakably her. I hung up immediately.

[ANGELA *enters.*]

ANGELA On Saturday morning we went to the hire shop in Cirencester to enquire about the flame-gun and a rotovator. Henry was cross and didn't want to go.

HENRY Why today?

ANGELA We keep putting it off.

HENRY It'll be hell on a Saturday.

ANGELA If I suggest going on Monday you'll say you're working.

HENRY We ought to get the car looked at.

ANGELA What's wrong with it?

HENRY The starter. I told you.

ANGELA I thought you'd had it mended.

HENRY I forgot.

ANGELA Please, Henry. The garden's in such a mess.

HENRY We can't do much now. It's the wrong time of the year.

ANGELA All we're talking about is clearing away the undergrowth and stuff. You can do that at any time.

HENRY There'll be nowhere to park.

[*He sits at his desk.*]

ANGELA Henry will never park illegally — not even for a couple of minutes, not even when it's perfectly safe and nobody cares. As it happened, there was a parking place right behind the shop. A nice young man called Steve showed us how to work the machines and told us there were daily, weekly or monthly hire arrangements. The monthly was easily the cheapest, so we opted for that.

[ANGELA *exits.*]

HENRY We haven't made love for several years. Five or six. There was no great severance or rift. It just stopped. I wonder how many men in their fifties are secret masturbators? Thousands, probably. Millions.

[JOANNA *enters.* HENRY *stands to greet her.*]

Welcome back.

JOANNA Thank you.

HENRY I've missed you.

JOANNA I've missed you.

HENRY I can't believe that.

JOANNA It was a long two weeks.

HENRY Did you have a good time?

JOANNA So-so. It rained a lot. Alexander ate a bad prawn. [*Pause.*] I've brought you a present. It's very silly. [*reaches into her handbag and produces a large stone*] I found it on the beach. I thought you could use it as a paperweight.

HENRY It's very beautiful. Thank you.

[*He kisses her fleetingly on the cheek.*]

Why don't we have lunch?

JOANNA When?

HENRY Tomorrow?

JOANNA Difficult tomorrow.

HENRY What about Thursday?

JOANNA Yes, all right.

HENRY Angela's going out. Some sort of cookery demonstration. We could drive somewhere.

JOANNA Drive where?

HENRY Where would you like to go?

JOANNNA I don't mind.

HENRY You choose.

JOANNA There's a place near Burford.

HENRY What place is that?

JOANNA Somebody was telling us. A hotel with a good restaurant. I'll find out, shall I?

HENRY Yes, do.

Warm sun.

HENRY   I took a B-road that led us through the most glorious countryside; and for miles, it seemed, there was nothing in sight, no cars, not even a farmhouse.

JOANNA   We listened to jazz.

HENRY   Ben Webster.

JOANNA   There was a field of yellow rape; a huge, sloping field of yellow rape. Henry stopped the car.

HENRY   Everything was buzzing with summer. It reminded me of my childhood. Staying with my grandmother in Kent. Running through bracken and long grasses. We got out of the car and stood side by side. I felt completely at ease with her.

JOANNA   Look down there.

HENRY   What?

JOANNA   That house. Do you see? Almost hidden by the trees. I wonder who lives there.

HENRY   We shall never know.

JOANNA   There's somebody moving by the window. I wonder what she's doing.

HENRY   Getting lunch, probably. It's half-past twelve.

JOANNA   I wonder if she's as happy as I am.

HENRY   Are you happy?

JOANNA   Tremendously.

HENRY   I wanted to take her in my arms.

JOANNA   I wanted him to hold me.

HENRY   I walked back to the car. 'Time to go,' I said.

JOANNA   Henry tried to start the car. It made a funny coughing noise.

HENRY   Nightmare. I could imagine it all. 'What were you doing there? Why were you taking her out to lunch? What's going on?'

JOANNA He got out and opened the bonnet. I went and stood beside him. We stared down into the engine.

HENRY I fiddled desperately with the leads and connections around the battery.

JOANNA What's wrong?

HENRY It must be the bloody starter. I should've got it fixed last week.

JOANNA There's oil on your shirt.

HENRY There's oil on my shirt because there's oil on my fingers.

JOANNA Don't be cross.

HENRY I am cross.

JOANNA We got back into the car. Henry tried again. The engine started. I'm not sure who was the more relieved, him or me.

HENRY Thank God for that.

JOANNA Well done.

HENRY Pure fluke. Sorry.

JOANNA For what?

HENRY For being bad-tempered.

JOANNA You weren't.

HENRY I was. I'm sorry.

We drove on. Joanna wanted to hear the Ben Webster tape again. She was wearing a linen skirt. The sun was warm. She was sitting with her legs apart. I longed to touch her.

JOANNA The hotel was a converted Georgian country house with Saabs and BMWs parked outside. Henry took my hand as we walked to the front door.

HENRY Don't be embarrassed. I gave a false name.

JOANNA What do you mean?

HENRY   When I booked the table they asked for my name and telephone number. I didn't want them ringing me at home.

[JOANNA *laughs.*]

You don't mind?

JOANNA   Why should I mind?

[BASSETT, *the hotel manager, enters.*]

BASSETT   Good morning, sir. Can I help you?

HENRY   Yes, my name's Stephenson. I booked a table for one o'clock.

BASSETT   Ah yes.

HENRY   I need to wash. The car went wrong. I'm covered in oil.

BASSETT   The cloakroom's downstairs, sir. Or would you rather have a shower?

HENRY   Is that possible?

BASSETT   Yes, sir, of course; I'm sure we can find you an empty room.

[BASSETT *exits.*]

JOANNA   The girl from the Reception Desk led us upstairs. She called me Mrs Stephenson and chatted about the weather. 'What a beautiful day,' she said. 'When it's warm and sunny like this I'd rather be in England than anywhere else in the world.'

HENRY   We went to room 14. I don't remember how it began or who made the first move.

JOANNA   There was no hesitation. We made love immediately.

HENRY   It was all over very quickly. We showered and dressed and had lunch.

[JOANNA *exits.*]

Evening. ANGELA *enters.*

ANGELA   How was your day?

HENRY Not bad. Well, not wonderful. The car broke down. I knew it would.

ANGELA What happened?

HENRY I went in to Cirencester to do some photocopying. Damn thing wouldn't start.

ANGELA Where were you?

HENRY Outside the bus station. Right in the middle of all the traffic.

ANGELA What did you do?

HENRY I fiddled about with the battery leads, then it started.

ANGELA You must take it to the garage.

HENRY Yes, I'll ring them.

[ANGELA *exits*.]

Day. JOANNA *enters*.

JOANNA We had coffee together the following afternoon. Henry and Angela were in the kitchen when I arrived for work. They'd just finished lunch. 'I'll make some coffee,' she said. I fetched the milk from the fridge.

HENRY Angela had arranged to take the car to the garage. Joanna and I went to the study. I heard the car drive away.

JOANNA How long will she be?

HENRY At least an hour.

JOANNA Goody.

HENRY She took off her pants and lay down on the sofa. I had no shame. She made me shameless.

JOANNA Angela got back at half-past four. At half-past five I switched off the computer and went home.

HENRY I won't see you again till Tuesday.

JOANNA I know.

HENRY I can't bear it.

JOANNA   What can we do?

HENRY   I'll ring Alexander.

           [ALEXANDER *enters*.]

           I'd like Joanna to work longer hours. Would that be
           a problem?

ALEXANDER Not as far as I'm concerned. What does she say?

HENRY   I haven't asked her actually. Is she there?

ALEXANDER She's gone shopping. I'm sure she wouldn't mind.

HENRY   I don't want to interfere with your domestic routine.

ALEXANDER She usually does household things in the morning.
           Why doesn't she come to you in the afternoon?

HENRY   You mean every afternoon?

ALEXANDER Why not?

           [ALEXANDER *exits*.]

HENRY   We made love whenever we could, wherever we
           could. On the sofa, on the floor, anywhere. Never in
           bed, of course — too much of a risk.

JOANNA   One day she came back from the shops earlier than
           expected. It was like a French farce, Henry tripping
           over his trousers, me looking for my pants, bump-
           ing into each other half undressed, Angela coming
           through the front door while I was pulling up my
           tights. It was ridiculously funny and sexy too.
           When Angela came in we were both laughing help-
           lessly.

           [ANGELA *enters*.]

ANGELA   What's the matter?

JOANNA   I made such a silly mistake. I typed bass-baritone
           — B–A–S–E.

           [*They all laugh*.]

HENRY   How easily she lied. How convincingly.

ANGELA   Would you like some tea?

JOANNA   That'd be lovely.

HENRY We had tea and home-made muffins. Angela asked Joanna if she knew anyone who could make curtains for us. Yes, said Joanna, there's a woman in the next village. They discussed the relative merits of different curtain fittings. I could smell her cunt on my fingers.

JOANNA These muffins are delicious.

ANGELA Take some home for Alexander.

[JOANNA *exits.*]

Evening. KATE *enters.*

KATE For the last few years we've spent Christmas together, Henry and Angela and me — and although it was only the first week of October, preliminary plans were discussed over Angela's *boeuf en daube à la niçoise.*

ANGELA It all depends on Ben, of course, whether or not he wants to come home.

HENRY I don't think he will.

ANGELA He might.

HENRY I doubt it.

KATE Let's work on the assumption that it'll be just the three of us.

ANGELA Right.

HENRY Where had you in mind?

KATE Somewhere abroad.

HENRY Sun or snow?

KATE Either. Both. What do you think?

ANGELA No strong feelings.

KATE Henry?

HENRY Up to you entirely. Entirely up to you.

[*The telephone rings.* JOANNA *enters.* ANGELA *answers the call.*]

ANGELA   Hello?

JOANNA   It's me, Jo. Sorry to bother you. Is Henry there?

ANGELA   Yes, hang on. It's Jo.

HENRY   Jo?

My stomach gave a nasty lurch. Had Alexander found out? Was he, at this very moment, on his way to confront me with my adulterous crimes?

[*He takes the receiver from* ANGELA.]

Joanna. What's the problem?

JOANNA   He's having a bath. I wanted to hear your voice.

KATE   Switzerland?

ANGELA   We can't ski.

KATE   Does that matter?

HENRY   Is something wrong?

JOANNA   I wish you weren't sitting there with Angela. All husband-and-wifey.

HENRY   It isn't like that.

KATE   Portugal. The Algarve.

ANGELA   I don't fancy Portugal.

KATE   What about Austria?

JOANNA   There's somebody talking. Who's talking?

HENRY   Kate's here.

ANGELA   Vienna might be nice. Christmas in Vienna.

JOANNA   What are you talking about?

HENRY   Christmas.

JOANNA   Are you going abroad?

HENRY   Possibly.

KATE   What about Italy? Florence?

ANGELA   I love Florence.

JOANNA   Don't go. Stay here.

HENRY   I wish I could.

ANGELA What are the winters like in Florence?

KATE Warmer than England.

JOANNA You'll go abroad and make love to her.

HENRY Of course I won't.

JOANNA Of course you will, you're bound to.

HENRY I won't, I promise I won't.

ANGELA What about Paris?

KATE Terribly expensive.

JOANNA I want you, Henry.

KATE I prefer Italy.

ANGELA Yes, so do I.

JOANNA I want you so much.

KATE Let's see what Henry thinks.

JOANNA I want you *now*.

HENRY I'm afraid that'll have to wait until tomorrow.

JOANNA I love you.

HENRY Yes, me too. Thanks for ringing.

[JOANNA *exits*. HENRY *hangs up*.]

KATE What about Florence?

HENRY What?

KATE Christmas in Firenze.

HENRY Very nice.

ANGELA Is Jo all right?

HENRY Yes, fine.

KATE What's Italian for Happy Christmas?

HENRY *Buon Natale*.

KATE Is it?

ANGELA He's guessing.

[KATE *exits*.]

Evening. Rain. ALEXANDER *and* JOANNA *enter and sit at a table.*

HENRY   Alexander was promoted to Deputy Head. This was a cause for celebration. He drove us to the Taj Mahal tandoori restaurant in Cheltenham. The weather was ghastly.

> [HENRY *and* KATE *enter and join them at the table.*]

ALEXANDER   Have some lamb tikka.

HENRY   Not for me, thanks.

ALEXANDER   What's the matter? I thought you liked Indian food?

HENRY   Nothing too hot.

ANGELA   He's hopeless with anything spicy.

ALEXANDER   Dear God —

HENRY   Doesn't matter.

ALEXANDER   — you should've said.

HENRY   Please don't worry about me.

ALEXANDER   We could've gone somewhere else.

HENRY   No, please —

ALEXANDER   Is the food all right for you?

ANGELA   Yes, lovely.

ALEXANDER   Jo — you look anguished. What's the matter?

JOANNA   Nothing.

ALEXANDER   Come on, let's all be cheerful. It's Alexander's Big Day.

ANGELA   Yes, well done, congratulations.

ALEXANDER   Actually, I was joking. It does seem extraordinary, don't you think, how the passage of time mocks our youthful aspirations?

HENRY   What do you mean?

ALEXANDER   Well, here we are — the four of us — gathered together to celebrate my appointment as Deputy Head of Westfield School. If someone had predicted (when

I was young and in my prime) that this would be the apogee of my professional life, I'd have laughed in his face — and/or jumped off the nearest cliff.

JOANNA You don't mean that.

ALEXANDER I certainly do. Good God, I had no wish to end my days as a schoolmaster.

ANGELA What did you want to do?

ALEXANDER I can't possibly tell you. It's too sad and too embarrassing. What about you, Henry? Aren't you sick to death of old gramophone records?

HENRY Well actually, no, not really.

ALEXANDER I can't believe that.

ANGELA Henry's always loved his work.

ALEXANDER I can't believe that fiddling about with woofers and tweeters was your idea of a full and richly satisfying life.

HENRY Well, it depends what you mean —

ALEXANDER Tell me the truth, Henry: what is your secret desire? A night with Greta Scacchi or Sigourney Weaver? — or would you prefer that girl in the photocopier's next to the bus station...?

JOANNA Do stop it, please.

ALEXANDER Stop what?

JOANNA You're drinking too much.

ALEXANDER I've had three beers.

JOANNA You know you can't drink.

ALEXANDER Thank you.

ANGELA I do like this restaurant. It's so much lighter than most Indian restaurants.

JOANNA That's because of the wallpaper.

ALEXANDER There isn't any.

JOANNA That's what I mean.

ALEXANDER The owner's a poof. Look at him. He's got dyed hair.

HENRY I think that's something to do with his religion.

ALEXANDER What do you mean?

HENRY It means he's been to Mecca.

ALEXANDER What are you talking about?

JOANNA Is that true?

HENRY I think so.

ALEXANDER Let's ask him.

JOANNA Please don't.

ANGELA What are you doing for Christmas?

[ANGELA, JOANNA *and* HENRY *exit.*]

California sun. BEN *enters.*

BEN One of Alice's friends knows Gerald Edelman — they worked together at the Scripps Institute. She knew I wanted to meet him, so a dinner party was arranged.

Apart from its scientific importance, Dr Edelman's work has profound moral implications. He argues that any investigation into the nature of consciousness should begin not with psychology or philosophy, but with biology. Since there is no aspect of human behaviour that cannot be accounted for by evolution, it's not unreasonable to suppose that the human mind is the result of evolutionary developments in the biological structure of the human brain. His ideas thus create a link between our physical existence and our so-called inner life — between neurology and the soul.

If we could accept that the spirit is as mortal as the flesh, then a new and richer morality could emerge: a morality that abandons supernatural myths and is based on values that are both more enlightened and more appropriately humane. This is what I wanted to discuss with Dr Edelman, but, alas, the dinner party didn't work out. There'd been a bad accident on the San Diego Freeway and Dr Edelman called to say that the traffic was impossible. He was charming and apologetic and said he hoped we'd get together at some future date.

When I got home I found a disconcerting message from my father on the answering machine.

[BEN *exits.*]

An autumn evening. Garden terrace. HENRY *and* KATE *enter.*

KATE   I gather you're having a busy time.

HENRY   Not specially.

KATE   Oh I thought you were. Angela said you're working extra hours with what's-her-name. Joanna.

HENRY   Oh yes.

KATE   How are you getting on with the book?

HENRY   Very well. Over halfway through.

KATE   When do you think you'll be finished?

HENRY   The point is — I'm in love with her. [*Pause.*] That's why I'm working extra hours.

[*Pause.*]

KATE   What?

HENRY   Joanna. I'm in love with Joanna. Oh Kate. What am I going to do?

KATE   Does she know how you feel?

HENRY   Yes.

KATE   Are you lovers?

HENRY   Yes.

KATE   For how long?

HENRY   About a month. Over a month.

KATE   What about Angela?

HENRY   She doesn't know.

KATE   And the husband?

HENRY   Alexander. He doesn't know either. Are you very surprised?

KATE   Yes.

HENRY   Shocked?

KATE   Surprised.

HENRY   I didn't mean to tell you.

KATE   I'm glad you did.

HENRY   Are you?

KATE   Yes, if it helps. Does it help?

HENRY   Yes.

KATE   How do you feel?

HENRY   Desperate. Bewildered. All this should've happened when I was seventeen. Why didn't it? Look at me, I've lost almost a stone.

KATE   Aren't you eating?

HENRY   Like a horse. My metabolism has changed. Everything's changed. I seem to have become an entirely different person. I even look different.

KATE   No, you don't.

HENRY   God, what a mess. I didn't intend to fall in love with her.

KATE   Nobody forced you to.

[HENRY *chooses to ignore this*.]

HENRY   I didn't even like her when I first met her. I thought she was irritating. Fey. She's not even pretty. God knows what'll happen when Angela finds out.

KATE   Perhaps she won't.

HENRY   Of course she will.

KATE   Not necessarily.

HENRY   I'm a moral man. I can't lead a double life. Anyway, she'll guess.

KATE   She may not.

HENRY Of course she will! We've been married for twenty-eight years. She *knows* me. I love her. I care for her very much. I don't want to hurt her. If we split up, it'll destroy her.

KATE It might not.

HENRY You know it will.

KATE It'll hurt her. It won't destroy her. People aren't destroyed like that.

HENRY Some are.

KATE Very few.

HENRY I wish she'd just disappear. I can't bear the idea of causing her pain.

KATE Sometimes pain can't be avoided.

HENRY God, I want a cigarette.

KATE How long have you known Joanna? It can't be more than a couple of months.

HENRY Since May. I've known her since the beginning of May. It's ridiculous. I mean — ridiculous. [*paces distractedly*] I'm possessed by her, Kate. I think of her all the time. Not 'think' — thinking's too organised — elation, lust, tenderness, guilt, excitement, despair — raw feelings, Kate, whirling around out of control. I mean, the other night — after we'd been to see you — we drove back past their house — there was a light in the bedroom window — well, why not, for God's sake? — it was eleven o'clock, it was bedtime, why shouldn't there be a light in their bedroom window? — and I thought of them getting undressed and going to bed together. It made me ill, Kate. Literally. I was sick. As soon as we got home, I rushed up to the bathroom and was violently, hideously sick. I was sweating and trembling. I was ill with jealousy. Physically ill. I told Angela it must've been your sherry trifle.

KATE   Thanks.

[HENRY *sinks onto a chair.*]

HENRY   I think perhaps I'm going mad.

KATE   Perhaps you are.

[*Once again,* HENRY *chooses to ignore his sister's tart response.*]

HENRY   It's just so awful. I don't know what to do.

KATE   Would you be angry if I used the word infatuation?

HENRY   No, you're right, I am infatuated, I know that. But it's something else. Something more. I feel I've been waiting for her all my life. I *am* infatuated, but that doesn't make it any the less real.

KATE   Depends what you mean by real.

HENRY   You mean is it real like my life with Angela is real? It's completely different. How can you judge one reality against another?

All my life I've either been looking back at happy times that have gone or looking forward to happiness to come. With Joanna, I'm happy *now*.

[HENRY *and* KATE *exit.*]

A sunny afternoon. The telephone rings. BEN *enters.* ANGELA *enters and answers the call.*

ANGELA   Hello?

BEN   Mum, it's Ben.

ANGELA   Ben!

BEN   How are you?

ANGELA   I'm fine. What a lovely surprise!

BEN   Sorry I didn't ring last weekend.

ANGELA   How are you?

BEN   Fine. Working hard.

ANGELA   How's California?

BEN Warm and wonderful. How's Dad?

ANGELA He's not here. He's gone to see Kate.

BEN Is he all right?

ANGELA Yes, very well. He'll be sorry to have missed you.

BEN He left a message on the answering machine.

ANGELA When was this?

BEN A couple of days ago. I was a bit worried.

ANGELA What about?

BEN Are you sure he's all right?

ANGELA What did he say?

BEN I couldn't hear all of it. It was sort of jumbled and confused. At the end he said, 'Don't think badly of me.'

ANGELA Don't think what?

BEN Don't think badly of me.

ANGELA What did he mean?

BEN I've no idea.

ANGELA Are you sure that's what he said?

BEN That's what it sounded like.

ANGELA I can't think what he was talking about.

BEN I was worried.

ANGELA Don't be. There's nothing to worry about.

BEN Are you sure?

ANGELA Absolutely. This new way of life seems to suit him.

BEN And what about you?

ANGELA Yes, I'm fine.

BEN Don't just say that, Mum. Tell me the truth. How are you?

ANGELA I'm fine.

BEN Really?

ANGELA *Really.* When are we going to see you?

BEN Soon — I'm not sure. Mum: I must go now. I'm using the clinic's phone. I'll call next week. Take care. Much love.

ANGELA And to you. Take care of yourself.

[BEN *exits.*]

When Henry came home we had a row about the garden. Well, not about the garden itself — about the rotovator and the flame-gun. We got them weeks ago and they're still sitting in the shed where we left them, unused and untouched. Apart from anything else, it's such a waste of money. 'I'll do it tomorrow,' he said. 'Always tomorrow,' I shouted at him, 'always tomorrow!' He just looked at me. He sulked for about an hour or so, and then went out in the garden and started clearing away the undergrowth.

He closes the bathroom door when he has a bath. He never used to. It started when we were living in London. Why do I find it so upsetting? I tried to talk to Ben about it, but he didn't want to know — why should he, after all? — it's not a good idea to talk to your children about those sort of things.

He doesn't even kiss me goodnight.

[ANGELA *exits.*]

A cloudy morning. HENRY *enters.*

HENRY Angela got up early. I lay in bed, pretending to be asleep. I heard her splashing about in the bathroom. I went downstairs and made a pot of coffee. All the cupboards and drawers were wide open. It's one of Angela's little foibles: she never shuts doors, she never shuts drawers. I spend my life shutting them after her.

[ANGELA *enters.*]

ANGELA I'm going to London.

HENRY   When?

ANGELA   Now. After breakfast. We must get some new sofa covers. I'm going to Peter Jones.

HENRY   What's wrong with the ones we've got?

ANGELA   They're too big.

HENRY   Too big ... ?

ANGELA   The pattern's too big. It was all right for London, but it's wrong here. We need something more delicate. If Peter Jones haven't got what I want, I'll try Laura Ashley, though I'm a bit bored with Laura Ashley. It won't cost too much, don't worry — Jo's lady who's making the curtains can make them and she's terribly inexpensive. There's a train at 4:35, so I'll be home about six.

[HENRY *goes to his desk and sits down.*]

HENRY   The prospect of a whole day with Joanna produced an immediate erection. I concealed my excitement by escaping to the study.

[ANGELA *puts on her coat and goes to* HENRY.]

ANGELA   There's some pâté and salad in the fridge. We'll have lamb chops tonight. Will that be all right?

HENRY   Yes, fine.

[ANGELA *kisses* HENRY *on the top of his head.*]

ANGELA   I'll see you later.

HENRY   About six.

ANGELA   About six.

[ANGELA *exits.*]

[HENRY *stands up.*]

HENRY   I telephoned Joanna. Alexander had already left for school. She was with me in thirty minutes.

[JOANNA *enters.*]

She lay on her side, naked, gazing towards the window. Her hand was pressed to her mouth. I loved the curve of her back: the faint, downy hair at the base of her spine.

What are you thinking?

JOANNA About going abroad. Going away with you. [*goes to him*] I was watching a plane. I was thinking of the passengers. Soon they'll be landing and waiting for their bags and getting taxis and going to hotels. I was thinking how wonderful it would be to go to a hotel with you. Somewhere warm and a long way away.

[*They embrace and kiss.*]

HENRY When I was a boy I used to lie on the grass and watch the planes going towards London airport. We always called it London airport in those days — never Heathrow. Sometimes I'd pick up a stick and aim it at the plane like a gun; and I used to think that the power of my imagination might be enough to make the plane blow up in a huge explosion of flames and smoke. One day a plane actually crashed — I heard it on the news. I was absolutely terrified. I thought I'd get the blame. I thought it was all my fault. I lived in terror for weeks. Every time I saw a policeman I trembled.

JOANNA What a funny creature you must've been.

HENRY Still am.

For the first time we made love in bed. My bed. Angela's bed. I pushed her body into positions that were deliberately lewd and salacious. 'I want to tie you to the bed,' I said. 'I want to tie you with your arms above your head and your legs wide open.' 'You can do anything you like,' she said. 'Anything you like.' I wanted it to last for ever. Nothing could ever be enough.

JOANNA We had lunch: pâté and salad and a glass of white wine.

[HENRY *pours wine for himself and* JOANNA.]

HENRY   When did you and Alexander last make love?

JOANNA   You shouldn't ask such a question.

HENRY   Why not?

JOANNA   You just shouldn't.

[*Pause. She sips her wine.*]

HENRY   Tell me.

JOANNA   You won't like it.

HENRY   When?

JOANNA   Last night.

[HENRY *looks at her. Pause.*]

HENRY   How often — I mean, how often ... ?

JOANNA   Depends. Twice a week. Thereabouts.

HENRY   Do you pretend to enjoy it?

JOANNA   I have to.

HENRY   God.

[*He sits down.*]

JOANNA   You shouldn't have asked.

HENRY   God.

[*He drinks his wine*]

We made love again. She slept in my arms.

She left at her usual time: half-past five. She phoned from the call box at the end of the road. 'I miss you already,' she said.

JOANNA   I miss you already.

[JOANNA *exits.*]

HENRY   I made some tea and had a slice of the cherry cake Angela had bought at the church fête. I made the bed, carefully checking that there were no tell-tale stains on the sheet. I had a quick shower and watched the television news: a political crisis in France and riots about something in Tokyo. At 6:30 I went into the kitchen and prepared vegetables for supper. I began listening for sounds of Angela's return. Car wheels on the gravel, her key turning in the lock. Nothing. At seven o'clock I poured myself a drink. A gin and tonic. I don't often do that. Then it occurred to me that she might have gone to see an old friend who lives in Chelsea, not far from Peter Jones. I telephoned the friend and spoke to her daughter who said she was looking after the house while her parents were on holiday in Tuscany. She had not seen Angela. I listened to the travel news on the radio, half expecting to hear reports of a serious accident or derailment. Nothing. I had another drink. I then spent half an hour trying to ring the railway station to see if there had been any delays or cancellations, but all I could get was one of those irritating recorded messages giving me the times of the trains. It seemed quite impossible to make contact with a live human being. I tried to read but couldn't concentrate. At ten o'clock I decided to phone the police.

END OF ACT ONE

ACT TWO

Morning. KATE *and* ALEXANDER.

ALEXANDER How is he?

KATE Asleep, I hope. He's upstairs — completely exhausted.

ALEXANDER What actually happened?

KATE Nobody knows. Angela didn't come home. Henry waited and waited, then he called the police.

ALEXANDER Then what?

KATE Some young police constable turned up and told him not to worry. Can you imagine anything more idiotic? Henry was up all night, of course, worrying himself sick. Another policeman came this morning — an inspector, I think he was.

ALEXANDER What did he say?

KATE Much the same. He asked a lot of questions.

ALEXANDER So we've no idea where she is?

KATE None.

ALEXANDER God.

KATE Presumably nothing too awful has happened. If there'd been an accident or something, we'd know about it.

ALEXANDER Would we?

KATE That's what the police said. And I can't believe she's been abducted in the middle of Peter Jones.

ALEXANDER So what do you think ... ?

KATE I don't know.

ALEXANDER Poor old Henry. He must be out of his mind.

KATE He is.

[*Pause.*]

ALEXANDER Perhaps she's gone off deliberately. Do you think she
      has? Perhaps she planned it.

KATE [*frowns*] Planned what?

        [ALEXANDER *shrugs, but says nothing; his silence
        is eloquent.*]

      Oh no. She wouldn't do a thing like that.

ALEXANDER Maybe not.

KATE She wouldn't just walk out. In any case — *why?*

ALEXANDER Who knows?

        [KATE *stares at him, astonished but not entirely
        sceptical.*]

KATE Do you think it's possible ... ?

ALEXANDER I don't know. I had a funny feeling something might
      be wrong.

KATE What do you mean?

ALEXANDER I couldn't put my finger on it. Henry didn't seem him-
      self. There was something about his manner. I said
      to Jo, 'I'm sure something's wrong,' I said, 'he seems
      preoccupied. Not himself.' Jo said I was talking non-
      sense. 'You're talking nonsense,' she said. Perhaps I
      wasn't. What d'you think?

        [*The doorbell rings.*]

      That might be her. She said she'd come round.

        [KATE *goes to the door. Detective-Inspector* CLIVE
        POOLE *enters: plain-clothes, in his forties.*]

POOLE Sorry to bother you again.

KATE No bother. Do come in. Inspector Poole, Mr Barley.

ALEXANDER How do you do.

POOLE How do you do, sir.

ALEXANDER Any news?

POOLE I'm afraid not.

KATE Henry's asleep. Do you want to talk to him?

POOLE I borrowed a photograph of Mrs Preece. I came

to return it. No need to disturb him. [*glances at* ALEXANDER] Your wife is Mr Preece's secretary — is that right?

ALEXANDER Yes.

POOLE Yes, I thought the name seemed familiar.

KATE So what happens now?

POOLE We're checking hospitals and accident reports. I'll speak to the Missing Persons Bureau at Scotland Yard.

KATE Did you check with Peter Jones?

POOLE We did. There's no record of her having bought anything; but that, of course, means very little. She may've gone there and not seen anything she liked.

ALEXANDER So now what?

POOLE We'll wait a couple of days. Most people come back within forty-eight hours.

ALEXANDER And if she doesn't ... ?

POOLE There's not a great deal we can do. If Mrs Preece chooses to leave home, that's her decision.

KATE I thought it was your job to look for missing people.

POOLE Only if there's suspicion of foul play — or if the missing person is under sixteen, elderly and in need of care, or mentally or physically handicapped. It's easy enough to find out if someone has died or been involved in an accident. If nothing like that has happened, we assume the person has gone missing because he or she wants to go missing. They're perfectly at liberty to do so. It's a free country, after all. Or so they say.

KATE So what's Henry supposed to do? Go out and look for her himself?

POOLE There are various organisations. I can give you the phone numbers. They all do remarkable work. At least seventy per cent of those who go missing are eventually found.

ALEXANDER What happens to the rest?

POOLE They start new lives. Presumably. It's not a crime to adopt another name, providing there's no intention to defraud.

ALEXANDER How extraordinary.

POOLE Yes, amazing, I agree. Somebody once worked out that the average person signs ten thousand official documents in the course of a lifetime. And yet it's still possible — surprisingly easy — to dodge under the curtain and to live a life totally free of tax codes, insurance numbers and other forms of bureaucratic bumf. I find that rather reassuring.

ALEXANDER Perhaps you wouldn't if it was *your* wife who had disappeared.

POOLE No, sir, I'm sure I wouldn't.

[HENRY *enters.*]

HENRY Good heavens. What a lot of people. Is there any news?

POOLE No, sir, I'm afraid not.

[HENRY *greets* KATE *with a kiss.*]

HENRY Isn't it time you went to work? You mustn't stay here on my account.

KATE I'll go in a minute.

ALEXANDER Dear old Henry, dear old boy. How are you feeling?

HENRY Odd. I ache all over, like flu.

ALEXANDER That's tension. The strain of it all.

[POOLE *takes an envelope from his pocket.*]

POOLE Your wife's photograph. I had some copies made.

HENRY Thank you.

[*The doorbell rings.*]

ALEXANDER Shall I go?

HENRY Yes, do.

[ALEXANDER *exits.*]

POOLE   You said Mrs Preece left home after breakfast. What time would that've been?

HENRY   Nine-ish. She caught the 9:43.

POOLE   Did you drive her to the station?

HENRY   She took a taxi.

POOLE   You rang for a taxi?

HENRY   I didn't, she did. Cotswold Minicabs. We always use them.

POOLE   Ah yes.

[ALEXANDER *enters with* JOANNA.]

ALEXANDER   This is my wife. Inspector Poole.

JOANNA   How do you do.

POOLE   How do you do.

JOANNA   Henry, I've been so worried...

[*She greets him with a kiss.*]

How are you?

HENRY   Not too bad.

[POOLE *turns to leave.*]

POOLE   I'll be in touch very shortly, Mr Preece.

JOANNA   Have you any idea what might've happened to her?

POOLE   Perhaps nothing. People sometimes have an irresistible desire to run away. They usually come back.

JOANNA   Run away from what?

POOLE   Obligations. Domesticity. Middle age.

HENRY   You mean she might be having some sort of nervous breakdown?

POOLE   I hate that phrase. So judgmental.

[*He shakes hands with* HENRY.]

Try not to worry, Mr Preece — I'll ring later. Good morning.

[*General 'good mornings' as* POOLE *exits.*]

ALEXANDER Well now, Henry, what are we going to do about you?

HENRY What do you mean?

ALEXANDER You can't stay here.

HENRY Why not?

KATE He can stay with me.

JOANNA He can stay with us.

HENRY No, no, no.

ALEXANDER You can't stay here on your own.

HENRY Why not?

ALEXANDER It's out of the question.

KATE Alexander's right. Come and stay with me.

HENRY How can I? Suppose something happens.

KATE We'll tell the police, give them my number, they can ring you there.

HENRY Angela might ring.

KATE We'll tell the exchange. They can divert calls. No arguments. Stay with me. [*turning to* ALEXANDER] I'm going to the office. Do you want a lift?

ALEXANDER Thank you.

KATE Jo?

JOANNA I'll stay and talk to Henry.

[KATE *kisses* HENRY.]

KATE Take care of yourself. I'll be home about seven.

[ALEXANDER *kisses* JOANNA.]

ALEXANDER I'll see you later. Usual time.

[*He grasps* HENRY *by the arm.*]

Dear old Henry. I so wish there was something I could do.

[KATE *and* ALEXANDER *exit. Pause.* JOANNA *and* HENRY *stand looking at each other.*]

JOANNA Where do you suppose she is?

HENRY I've no idea.

JOANNA Do you think she found out about us?

HENRY I don't know.

JOANNA She must've done.

HENRY Not necessarily.

JOANNA She must have. That's why she's doing this.

HENRY What do you mean?

JOANNA To punish us.

HENRY I don't think she has found out. She seemed perfectly all right when she left. Perfectly normal.

JOANNA What do the police say?

HENRY They keep telling me not to worry. Apparently most people come back within forty-eight hours.

JOANNA Perhaps she will.

HENRY Perhaps she's dead.

JOANNA Oh Henry, of course she's not.

HENRY How do you know?

JOANNA She can't be!

HENRY If she is, it's my fault.

JOANNA What do you mean?

HENRY I don't know. Pay no attention. I'm talking nonsense.

JOANNA What are you going to do?

HENRY I've no idea. I hadn't thought. Nothing, I suppose.

[HENRY *goes to the table and sits down.* JOANNA *exits.*]

California sun. BEN *enters.*

BEN After the initial shock, my immediate thoughts were almost entirely selfish. For one thing, Alice and I had arranged to spend the weekend with friends in Carmel. That was now in severe jeopardy. Then there was Dad. He sounded so helpless on the phone, and it made me realise that he's becoming an old man.

I'd always imagined that he and Mum would grow
old together: I suppose I envisaged some trouble-
free, gentle fading into a peaceful Gloucestershire
sunset. Quite clearly that was not going to be the
case. I just couldn't accept the fact that my mother
had disappeared in mysterious circumstances. It
seemed inconceivably bizarre. Mum's one of the
least mysterious people I've ever known. I felt sure
that there must be a reasonable explanation and
every time the phone rang I thought it'd be Dad
saying all was well, she was back, nothing to worry
about. No such luck. I booked myself a seat on
BA 268.

[BEN *exits.*]

Evening. KATE *enters and goes to the table where* HENRY
is sitting. They eat supper.

HENRY I rang Ben.

KATE What did he say?

HENRY Very upset. He wants to come over for a few days. Is
it all right if he stays here?

KATE Of course.

HENRY He'll be arriving tomorrow, early evening. Is that all
right?

KATE Yes, of course.

[*Pause. They eat.*]

HENRY Looking back, thinking things over — me and Joanna
— it really was a kind of madness.

KATE Yes.

HENRY Really.

KATE Yes.

HENRY I lost control. So did she. For a time, we shared some
kind of passionate insanity. [*looks at* KATE] You don't
know what I'm talking about.

KATE   Henry, you're not unique. You're not even particularly unusual. You may like to think you are, but you're not. I know exactly what you're talking about.

HENRY   How can you?

KATE   I had a lover for almost eighteen years.

HENRY   *You* did ... !

KATE   Don't sound so surprised.

HENRY   Who was it?

KATE   Bill. William Burgess. The senior partner.

HENRY   He's your lover?

KATE   Was. Yes.

HENRY   But he must be ...

KATE   What?

HENRY   He's an old man.

KATE   Twenty years older than me.

HENRY   Why did you never say anything?

KATE   He didn't want me to. I always did what he wanted.

HENRY   He's married.

KATE   Was.

HENRY   We met his wife. There was an office party. We were staying with you.

KATE   Christmas five years ago.

HENRY   What happened?

KATE   His wife died. I suppose I assumed we'd get married, but he didn't want that. He avoided talking about it. He saw me less often. Then one day he said we should stop seeing each other. Three months later he married somebody else.

HENRY   God.

KATE   I behaved very badly.

HENRY   I'm not surprised.

KATE   I rang them in the middle of the night. I threw stones at their bedroom window. I pushed dog shit through the letterbox. He threatened to call the police.

HENRY When was this?

KATE Last year.

HENRY I had no idea. We never even guessed.

KATE Angela caught me crying once. I said my cat had died.

HENRY You haven't got a cat.

KATE Angela didn't know that. Or if she did, she'd forgotten.

HENRY You should've told me.

KATE I told no one.

HENRY Poor Kate.

KATE That's why I didn't say anything. 'Poor Kate.' I didn't want to be pitied. Change the subject.

> [*Pause.*]

HENRY He asked me the colour of her eyes. Inspector Poole. I couldn't remember.

KATE What else did he ask you?

HENRY What was she wearing, had we quarrelled. It was very odd.

KATE Yes, I'm sure.

HENRY Like taking part in somebody else's life.

KATE Did you say anything about Joanna?

HENRY No. Say what about Joanna?

KATE About you and her.

HENRY No. Do you think I should've done?

KATE No, no, of course not.

HENRY Obviously you do —

KATE I don't.

HENRY — otherwise you wouldn't have mentioned it.

KATE I don't. Truly.

> [*Pause.*]

HENRY I keep thinking of what I said to you.

KATE What was that?

HENRY 'I wish she'd disappear.'

KATE When did you say that?

HENRY When I told you about Joanna.

KATE I don't remember.

HENRY We were talking about Angela finding out. I said I couldn't bear the thought of causing her pain. Then I said, 'I wish she'd just disappear.' Well, now she has.

KATE This is not your fault.

HENRY How do you know?

KATE Don't start blaming yourself.

HENRY I meant what I said. I wanted her out of the way. Out of my life. Without pain or problems or unpleasantness. Now I've got my wish.

KATE Don't talk nonsense, Henry. First of all, we don't know what's happened to her. She may be perfectly all right. Secondly, you're behaving as if you've committed a major crime. It's scarcely even a misdemeanour — just a brief moral lapse. Thirdly, it's incredibly self-centred to take all the blame yourself. There are other people involved in this.

HENRY Like who?

KATE Well, me for one.

HENRY You ... ? What've you got to do with it?

KATE I'm fond of her. She is my sister-in-law, after all. I should've done something when you told me what was going on.

HENRY Done what?

KATE I should've talked to her.

HENRY What good would that've done?

KATE Who knows? It might've done a lot of good. Anyway, I should've done something. I feel badly that I didn't.

[HENRY *is silent for a moment.*]

HENRY   Do you remember a boy called Alderton? Geoffrey
        Alderton.

KATE   Alderton ... ?

HENRY   We were at school together. Tall boy, ginger hair, lived
        near the golf course. We often walked home together
        past that toy shop near the Catholic church. Do you
        remember it? There was always a model train lay-
        out in the window: very elaborate, tunnels, stations,
        bridges, and all those trains rushing round and round
        on the circular track — goods trains, passenger trains,
        everything, it was marvellous.

KATE   Yes, I remember.

HENRY   One day, Geoffrey went into the shop. He waited until
        he saw the shopkeeper talking to a customer, then he
        went into the shop and stole a model engine. It was a
        Hornby-Dublo 'Schools' class locomotive in Southern
        Railways green. I can see it now. He just picked it up
        and walked out. Nobody saw him, nobody came run-
        ning after him, his parents never asked him where
        this new toy had come from. He simply got away with
        it; totally and completely got away with it.

        From that moment on, I was afraid of him. Not because
        I was afraid of being blamed or somehow implicated in
        his crime, but because he'd shown me that you could
        break the rules and get away with it. I found that very
        disturbing.

        He dropped dead at a Rotary Club lunch. Only forty-
        eight. Some sort of delayed retribution, perhaps.

        [*Lights fade on* HENRY *and* KATE.]

POOLE *enters.*

POOLE   A man called Bassett rang and asked to speak to
        me. He introduced himself as the manager of the
        Glebe Court Hotel, near Burford. I know it well. My

wife and I have formed the habit of celebrating our
wedding anniversary there. Excellent wine list.

[*Lights on* BASSETT.]

BASSETT It's about this lady who disappeared ...

POOLE Mrs Preece?

BASSETT There's a photograph in the paper.

POOLE Yes?

BASSETT Well, the man with her — her husband — I think I
recognise him.

POOLE Perhaps he came to the hotel.

BASSETT Yes, but he was using a different name.

[*Lights fade on* BASSETT *and* POOLE.]

Afternoon. HENRY *enters.*

HENRY Kate went to work. It was, after all, just another day.
I didn't know what to do. I sat down and switched
on the television. A fat lady was advising people
about their sexual problems. That was followed by a
discussion on hormone replacement therapy. That
was followed by a quiz show. That was followed by a
Bugs Bunny cartoon. On another channel there was
an American puppet show with strange woolly
creatures that looked like brightly coloured cater-
pillars. That was followed by an old film with Rex
Harrison. On another channel there was a pro-
gramme about politics. That was followed by a film
about a railway in Ecuador.

[JOANNA *enters.*]

JOANNA What are you doing?

HENRY Well, nothing.

JOANNA I thought you'd ring.

HENRY Sorry.

JOANNA Why didn't you?

HENRY   I wasn't quite sure ...

JOANNA   What?

HENRY   Whether we should meet or not.

JOANNA   What do you mean?

HENRY   I thought perhaps we should be — you know — a bit careful for a day or so.

JOANNA   Why?

HENRY   Just in case somebody started jumping to conclusions.

JOANNA   Why should they?

HENRY   I don't know.

> [JOANNA *goes to him.*]

JOANNA   I need you, Henry. I need to be with you.

> [*They are about to embrace when* BEN *enters. He is carrying a canvas travelling bag.* HENRY *springs away from* JOANNA.]

HENRY   Ben!

BEN   Dad — it's good to see you.

> [BEN *puts down his bag. He goes to* HENRY *and embraces him.*]

HENRY   We didn't think you'd be here till much later.

BEN   I caught an earlier plane.

HENRY   This is Joanna, Mrs Barley, my, uh — one of our neighbours.

BEN   Hello.

JOANNA   Hello.

BEN   Any news of Mum?

HENRY   'fraid not.

> [JOANNA *turns to leave.*]

JOANNA   I'll ring you later, Henry.

BEN   Don't let me drive you away.

JOANNA   I have to get back home.

BEN You're the lady who's been helping with the book.

JOANNA That's right.

BEN How's it going?

JOANNA Very well. [*to* HENRY, *as she goes*] I'll talk to you later.

HENRY Please do.

JOANNA [*smiles at* BEN] I hope I see you again.

BEN I hope so too.

[JOANNA *exits. Pause.*]

So — no news ... ?

HENRY Nothing.

BEN What do the police say?

HENRY Not very much. You'd better talk to them yourself. I told them you were coming home.

BEN What exactly are they doing?

HENRY The police? I don't know. Asking questions, I suppose. Checking hospitals. Waiting for her to show up somewhere.

BEN [*looks at* HENRY] Do you think she's still alive?

HENRY I don't know.

BEN What do you *feel*?

HENRY I don't know. How about you?

BEN I can't believe she's dead. It doesn't seem possible. On the other hand ...

HENRY What?

BEN I can't believe it was all premeditated and planned. She sounded so completely normal when I spoke to her.

HENRY Perhaps she's lost her memory. Is that possible? — I mean, medically possible?

BEN Possible, yes.

HENRY How does it happen? Why?

BEN   There's a condition called hysterical fugue. An extreme
       form of memory loss and disassociation. A person
       suddenly switches off his or her normal identity —
       rather like changing TV channels. Uncommon in
       women of Mum's age, but it does happen.

HENRY Why — does anyone know?

BEN   Some people do it to avoid a painful situation; some
       do it to gain sympathy. Impossible to generalise.

HENRY Do they recover?

BEN   Oh yes. It all comes back slowly, bit by bit. But the
       missing days or weeks usually remain missing. That
       part they can't — or won't — remember.

                        [*Pause.*]

HENRY When did you last speak to her?

BEN   Saturday.

HENRY What time?

BEN   Just after breakfast. About four o'clock your time.
       She said you'd gone to see Kate.

HENRY She didn't tell me.

BEN   Perhaps she forgot.

HENRY It's most unlike her to forget. She always tells me
       when you ring.

BEN   [*hesitates*] Perhaps she decided not to.

HENRY Why should she do that?

BEN   I rang her about you.

HENRY About *me* ... ?

BEN   I was worried.

HENRY What about?

BEN   You left a very peculiar message on my answering
       machine.

HENRY Did I? [*remembers*] Oh yes.

BEN   I rang Mum to see if you were all right.

[HENRY *turns from him.*]

HENRY I had to tell him about Joanna. There was no way of avoiding it. My mouth went dry. I searched desperately for the right words.

BEN Of course I knew how unhappy she was.

[HENRY *stares, amazed.*]

HENRY What ... ?

BEN She wrote me a letter. And we talked on the phone.

HENRY When was this?

BEN When you were still in London. I knew how important it was, moving to the country.

HENRY Important ... ?

BEN For her. I tried to tell her you can't change your life by moving house, but she wouldn't listen. My one last chance, she called it.

[BEN *looks at* HENRY, *who remains silent.*]

You were aware of how she felt?

HENRY [*managing to make the lie convincing*] Yes, of course. Absolutely.

BEN I'm not blaming you for any of this, don't think that. These things happen, after all. Happiness comes and goes. It must've been tough for both of you.

[*No response.* BEN *picks up his bag.*]

I'll take this upstairs. Do you think Kate'd mind if I had a bath?

HENRY No, no, of course not.

[BEN *exits with his travelling bag.*]

I was stunned by what he said. I thought of all the days and weeks and months and years I'd lain beside her in bed. I'd had no idea what was passing through her mind. How is that possible?

[*Lights fade.*]

Evening.

HENRY The evening seemed endless. Ben talked about his work. Kate asked a lot of questions. I found conversation impossible. I was overwhelmed by feelings of sadness and regret and remorse. Nobody seemed to notice. Eventually Kate and Ben went to bed. I watched television. A comedy series about geriatrics. A documentary about Pakistanis in Bradford. Recorded highlights of a golf championship in Florida. I thought about Angela. I wept. The television programmes came to an end. I fell asleep on the sofa.

Day. POOLE *enters.*

POOLE There was a report of your wife's disappearance in the local paper.

HENRY Yes, I saw it.

POOLE We had a telephone call from Mr Bassett, the manager of a hotel near Burford. The Glebe Court Hotel.

HENRY Oh yes?

POOLE He saw your photograph in the paper and remembered you'd had lunch there. Apparently there was some trouble with your car.

HENRY Yes.

POOLE There was a lady with you.

HENRY Yes.

POOLE Would that have been your wife?

HENRY No, as a matter of fact — no.

POOLE He said you made the lunch reservation in the name of Stephenson. Is that correct?

HENRY Yes.

POOLE Why did you do that, sir?

HENRY Does it matter?

POOLE I just wondered if it might have some bearing on your wife's disappearance.

[*A momentary hesitation.*]

HENRY She knew nothing about it.

POOLE About what?

HENRY I've been having an affair. Well, I wasn't then. I wasn't when we had lunch at the hotel. Well, I was, I suppose. That's when it started. I don't know why I gave a false name. I must've had a reason. I forget.

POOLE The lady you had lunch with ... ?

HENRY Do I have to tell you her name?

POOLE Not if you'd rather not.

HENRY I'd rather not.

POOLE When did you have this lunch at the Glebe Court Hotel?

HENRY August. End of August.

POOLE So it's been going on for some time? The affair. Some months.

HENRY Just over two months.

POOLE Almost three.

HENRY That's not very long.

POOLE Long enough for your wife to find out.

HENRY I'm sure she didn't.

POOLE It would certainly make her disappearance more understandable. Wouldn't you say?

HENRY Possibly. Yes. I don't know.

POOLE Money problems, the breakdown of a relationship — particularly a long-standing relationship — they're the most common reasons for people to go missing.

HENRY Our 'relationship', as you call it, had not 'broken down'. We had a good marriage. On the whole.

POOLE A good marriage. What does that mean?

HENRY   Well ...

POOLE   The question was rhetorical, sir. No answer expected. 'Good' — such a confusing word.

HENRY   I wouldn't have said so.

POOLE   I had a good breakfast this morning. Does that mean that the breakfast was upright and virtuous; or that it did me good to consume the breakfast; and by that do I mean it was wholesome and nutritious or just pleasantly palatable?

What is truth and what is fable?
Where is Ruth and who is Mabel?

[*The doorbell rings.* HENRY *does not move.*]

Go ahead, sir. Answer the door.

HENRY   Yes.

[ALEXANDER *enters. He sees* POOLE.]

ALEXANDER   Oh — sorry. Is this a bad moment?

POOLE   No, sir, not at all.

ALEXANDER   Any news?

POOLE   I'm afraid not.

ALEXANDER   Would you rather I came back later?

POOLE   No, it's all right, sir, I was on the point of leaving. [*starts to exit but pauses*] It's an unusual name, Barley. Don't think I've come across it before.

ALEXANDER   Old English, found chiefly in Lancashire and Cheshire.

POOLE   Aha. We'll be in touch, Mr Preece.

HENRY   Yes, goodbye.

POOLE   Goodbye, sir.

ALEXANDER   Goodbye.

[POOLE *exits.*]

ALEXANDER   You're sure I wasn't interrupting?

HENRY   No, no. He just came round to — to check a few details.

ALEXANDER So they're still looking for her?

HENRY They're making enquiries.

[ALEXANDER *takes* HENRY *by the arm.*]

ALEXANDER How are you? How are you feeling?

HENRY Much the same.

ALEXANDER Eating properly?

HENRY Yes.

ALEXANDER Sleeping?

HENRY Yes, fine, more than usual.

ALEXANDER That's depression.

HENRY What is?

ALEXANDER Sleep as a means of escape. What you need is a change of scene. Something to occupy your mind.

HENRY I'll be all right.

ALEXANDER Now look: Jo and I are going down to my brother's next week. Why don't you come with us?

HENRY Oh no.

ALEXANDER Ben will have gone back. There's no point in moping about here all by yourself.

HENRY No, really, I couldn't.

ALEXANDER He lives near Lyme Regis. Beautiful. Just what the doctor ordered: a couple of days by the sea.

HENRY You're very kind.

ALEXANDER He'd be delighted to see you.

HENRY No, honestly —

ALEXANDER Why not?

HENRY I couldn't.

ALEXANDER Why not?

HENRY It's just impossible.

ALEXANDER Rubbish.

HENRY I'm sorry.

ALEXANDER   Henry: you're a good chap and we're both very fond
            of you. I know you're going through an extremely
            difficult and traumatic time — but you must do some-
            thing to help yourself. Stop being such an old stick-
            in-the-mud. It'd do you the world of good to get away
            for a couple of days. The police can keep an eye on
            things. You can drive down with us. All you've got
            to do is pack a bag. Come on, Henry — what do you
            say?

HENRY   I'm having an affair with Joanna.

              [*Pause.*]

ALEXANDER   What?

HENRY   Don't ask me to repeat it.

ALEXANDER   You're having an affair with Joanna?

HENRY   Yes.

ALEXANDER   Jesus Christ.

HENRY   I'm sorry.

ALEXANDER   You! *You* are having an affair with Joanna?

HENRY   I'm sorry. I'm sorry.

ALEXANDER   You're mad. You're ill. I don't believe it.

HENRY   It's true.

ALEXANDER   You're screwing my wife!

HENRY   Don't say that. Please.

ALEXANDER   Jesus Christ. God.

HENRY   I'm sorry.

ALEXANDER   You bastard.

HENRY   I had to tell you. The police are asking questions.

ALEXANDER   What do you mean?

HENRY   They know I've been having an affair. They found out.

ALEXANDER   How long has this been going on?

HENRY   September.

ALEXANDER   You bastard.

HENRY I'm sorry.

ALEXANDER When did you do it?

HENRY When we could.

ALEXANDER Where?

HENRY At home, my home.

ALEXANDER What about Angela?

HENRY When she was out.

ALEXANDER You said you wanted to work extra hours.

HENRY Yes.

ALEXANDER You were screwing my wife.

HENRY Yes.

ALEXANDER God, I should've guessed. What a fool, what an idiot! — God, you must've laughed.

HENRY I'm sorry.

ALEXANDER Does she love you?

HENRY I don't know.

ALEXANDER Of course you know! Does she say she loves you?

HENRY Please stop this.

ALEXANDER Tell me.

HENRY Yes.

ALEXANDER She says she loves you?

HENRY Yes.

ALEXANDER Oh God.

HENRY I'm sorry.

ALEXANDER Oh God. Oh God. Oh God.

[*He falls to his knees, weeping.*]

HENRY This is dreadful.

ALEXANDER Does she want to leave me?

HENRY No — no, nothing like that.

ALEXANDER You're lying. If she loves you, she wants to be with you. I know her. I know what she's like. I've lived with her all these years. Eleven years, for Christ's sake! Oh God.

HENRY   Stop it, please.

ALEXANDER   Why are you doing this? Why did you tell me?

HENRY   The police have been asking questions. I didn't want you to find out that way. I had to tell you.

ALEXANDER   You wanted to hurt me.

HENRY   No.

ALEXANDER   Liar.

HENRY   It's the truth.

ALEXANDER   Did Angela know? Did you tell her?

HENRY   No.

ALEXANDER   Is that why she left?

HENRY   No.

ALEXANDER   Liar.

HENRY   She didn't know, I'm sure she didn't know.

ALEXANDER   You destroy her life — you destroy mine. Bastard. I hope you rot in hell. I hope you die in agony.

[ALEXANDER *exits.*]

[*Pause.*]

HENRY   I saw his distress, but as if through a translucent screen. I was distanced from it. I felt nothing. I sat very still and watched it grow dark.

Late afternoon. JOANNA *enters.*

JOANNA   Why did you do that? Why did you tell him?

HENRY   I had to. The police are asking questions.

JOANNA   What about?

HENRY   Me having an affair.

JOANNA   Oh God.

HENRY   I haven't told them your name, but I may have to.

JOANNA   He's devastated. It's awful.

HENRY I know.

JOANNA He can't stop crying.

HENRY Does he know you're here?

JOANNA Yes, of course.

HENRY What did you say?

JOANNA I said I had to see you.

HENRY What did he say?

JOANNA Nothing. [*Pause.*] I'll have to stay with him. I can't leave —

HENRY No, no ...

JOANNA — I can't leave him when he's like this.

HENRY No, of course not.

JOANNA Why did you do it, Henry? Why did you tell him?

HENRY I had no choice.

JOANNA Angela might come back at any minute. Ben's here. You should've waited.

HENRY I couldn't.

[*Pause.*]

JOANNA Forgive me.

HENRY Nothing to forgive.

JOANNA I can't leave *now*.

HENRY I know.

JOANNA I'm sorry.

[HENRY *goes to her.*]

HENRY If it's any comfort, I didn't expect you to leave.

JOANNA What do you mean?

HENRY I never thought it was a real possibility.

[JOANNA *frowns, startled by this disclosure.*]

JOANNA What ... ?

HENRY I mean — not *real*.

JOANNA But I thought — it's what we both wanted — you said so ...

HENRY   Well, yes ...

JOANNA   Being together.

HENRY   Well, of course.

JOANNA   [*stares at him*] You didn't mean it.

HENRY   I did — absolutely.

JOANNA   You don't want me to leave ...

HENRY   Not now, no, it wouldn't be right.

JOANNA   You still love *her.*

HENRY   I love you.

JOANNA   No, you don't.

HENRY   Of course I do. You know I do.

JOANNA   Don't say it if you don't mean it.

HENRY   I do mean it.

JOANNA   You don't, you don't! — I can see you don't. You still love *her!*

> [HENRY *moves to embrace her.*]

HENRY   Joanna —

JOANNA   Keep away! [*thrusts him aside*] You're everything to me! Don't you understand that? I love you! You're my life! I feel sick. I'm going to be sick.

> [JOANNA *exits.* HENRY *sinks onto a chair.*]

POOLE *enters.*

POOLE   I decided to have another look at Mr Preece's cottage. Just to refresh my memory. Although it's only a few hundred metres from the village, it's surprisingly isolated. Not another house in sight. Everything was carefully locked and bolted. Mr Preece is clearly a methodical man. He's also a keen gardener: the shed was full of tools and gadgets — including a fearsome-looking flame-gun from the hire shop in Cirencester. There was a shelf of gardening books amongst which I found a small collection of bondage magazines. At the bottom of the garden I noticed a trench full of ashes. I thought of the flame-gun. I took some of the ashes away to be analysed.

[*He exits.*]

BEN *enters.*

BEN I went to London to see Gillian. We'd been students together and had a brief but very erotic affair. She's now married with three children and living what seems to be a parody of suburban life in south London. I enquired if she still took an interest in neuropsychology. 'Good Lord, no,' she said, 'all that's a thing of the past, I'm far too busy with the children.' She made me feel as if my question was in slightly bad taste. I guessed that eroticism had also become a thing of the past.

[*Lights fade.*]

Evening.

BEN The thought of supper with Dad depressed me. I had steak and chips in a cafe near the station and planned to go straight to bed when I got home, using a sudden onrush of jet lag as a (not unreasonable) excuse. [*takes off his raincoat*] I could hear the TV in the sitting room. My heart sank.

[HENRY *goes to him.*]

HENRY Hello, Ben. How was your day?

BEN Fine. Very pleasant. How was yours?

HENRY Fine. Uneventful.

BEN No news from the police?

HENRY Not a word.

BEN [*yawns*] God, I'm tired. Absolutely exhausted. I think I'll go to bed, if that's all right with you.

HENRY Have a drink first.

BEN I couldn't, Dad, really. I'm totally knackered. Must be jet lag.

HENRY Ben, please: I have to talk to you. It's very important.

BEN What is ... ?

HENRY Have a drink.

BEN I don't want a drink. What's the problem?

HENRY [*hesitates*] When you told me about Mum being unhappy, I lied. I had no idea.

BEN [*stares, astonished*] Why didn't you say ... ?

HENRY I couldn't. Wait. There's something else. There's something I have to tell you. [*Another hesitation.*] The point is, Ben — I know you're tired, but I have to tell you — you see, the point is, it's all my fault —

BEN What is?

HENRY Everything ...

BEN What?

HENRY I've been having an affair. [*Pause.*] I should've told you before. I wanted to. I didn't have the courage. I'm sorry.

BEN Did Mum know?

HENRY I can't be sure. I thought not.

BEN She must've done.

HENRY Nothing was said.

BEN She must've found out.

HENRY Yes, I suppose so. [*Pause.*] Are you very angry?

BEN I don't know what I am.

HENRY Tell me the truth. Please don't pretend.

BEN I'm not.

HENRY It's pointless coming six thousand miles and not telling me how you feel.

[BEN *is silent.*]

You must think I'm to blame —

BEN How long have you — ?

HENRY — you *must* — in your heart —

BEN Is this why you left that message on my answering machine?

HENRY Yes. [*Pause.*] Yes, I — I was lying in bed. Angela was asleep. I worked myself into a colossal panic. I knew I was going to be found out — but how, when, what would happen? I imagined the scenes and the tears and the recriminations. Then I thought of Angela telling you and I knew she wouldn't give me the chance to explain my side of things — why should she? — and I felt I had to talk to you, I had to say something, so I rang and left that ridiculous message. It was the middle of the night, don't forget, and I was half asleep. I'm sorry.

　　　　　[*Pause.*]

BEN Who is it?

HENRY Joanna.

　　　　　[BEN, *unsurprised, nods.*]

BEN I think I will have a drink after all.

　　　　　[*He looks around for the drinks;* HENRY *points to the appropriate table.*]

HENRY Over there ...

　　　　　[BEN *pours himself a whisky and drinks it quickly.*]

BEN Where's Kate?

HENRY Having dinner with friends.

　　　　　[BEN *goes to the door.*]

BEN I think I'll have a bath.

　　　　　[HENRY *seizes him by the arm.*]

HENRY Don't go. Please don't go.

BEN There's nothing more to say.

HENRY Oh but there is — please — there is.

　　　　　[BEN *pauses.*]

The point is — I couldn't stop it. The affair. Some evenings I'd sit at home, looking at Angela, and I'd think, my God, what am I doing? and I'd try to stop it — in my head — but I couldn't. It was very powerful. Physically. You understand? Physically it was the most powerful —

BEN Yes, all right.

HENRY Don't turn away. Let me explain.

BEN I don't want to hear this.

HENRY Please, you must listen, it's important that you understand —

BEN I'm going upstairs.

HENRY I don't want you to think I was just fooling around.

BEN I don't care what you were doing.

HENRY What do you mean?

BEN What's done is done; spare me the post mortem.

HENRY You *are* angry.

BEN I do not want to hear your sexual confessions.

HENRY I'm just trying to explain —

[BEN *turns from him abruptly.*]

BEN I've heard enough. I'm tired. I'm going to bed.

HENRY Please try to understand, Ben. I'm a human being in total confusion. You know about these things. I don't understand what's going on inside my head. I need someone to help me.

BEN Well, not me, I'm afraid. You're not a human being, you're my father. Fathers don't fuck the next-door neighbour. They live at home with Mum; they mow the lawn, pay the bills and live happily ever after. I'll see you in the morning.

[BEN *exits. Pause.* HENRY *pours himself a gin and tonic. He sits down.*]

KATE *enters.*

KATE   I'd been having dinner with my friends, the Olivers of Norris Wood. When I got home I found Henry drunk and snoring on the sofa. I woke him and he went to bed. I asked Ben what had happened. 'Nothing happened,' he said, 'I was tired. I went to bed early.' He asked if he could phone Los Angeles. I heard him telling someone that he'd decided to go back earlier than expected. 'There's nothing I can do here,' he said.

[KATE *exits.*]

ALEXANDER *enters.*

ALEXANDER   The weekend came and went. Jo slept in the spare room. The fact that she stayed in the house was an encouraging sign, if nothing else. At morning assembly we sang 'As pants the hart for cooling streams.' I love that hymn. We sang it often at school when I was a boy.

> [*sings*] As pants the hart for cooling streams
> When heated in the chase,
> So longs my soul, O God, for Thee,
> And Thy refreshing grace.

[ALEXANDER *exits.*]

BEN *enters.*

BEN   I spoke to Inspector Poole and told him I was going back to L.A. He seemed to think that my mother was most probably alive and had left because of my father's affair with Mrs Barley, which he knew about — guessed, anyway. He promised to keep me posted about any further developments. I couldn't wait to get out of the house. My father followed me from room to room, looking anxious and apologetic.

[HENRY *approaches* BEN.]

HENRY   What time's your flight?

BEN   Half-past four. I told you.

HENRY   You don't want to be late. There's a train about eleven. I'd aim for that if I were you, just to be on the safe side. Then you can get a train straight from Paddington to Heathrow.

[BEN *turns to* HENRY.]

BEN   For God's sake, Dad — don't do this to me!

HENRY   Don't do what?

BEN   Don't try to pretend that everything's back to normal. It's so fucking typical!

HENRY   What is?

BEN   Mum once said that every time she wanted to have a serious talk with you, you always started plumping up cushions or closing drawers. Typical.

[HENRY *stands very still, staring, aghast, at his son.*]

Something dreadful has happened. Something appalling. It'll change both of our lives for ever. And if it doesn't then it's all meaningless, her life, her death, everything.

HENRY   I'm sorry.

BEN   And stop blaming yourself. OK, it's partly your fault — at least, it may be — but you're not the only one. What about me? I should've helped her, I should've done something. She told me she was unhappy — I did bugger-all about it. I used California as an excuse. 'Can't do anything out here, I'm too far away.' I turned my back on her. How do you think I feel about that? Don't be so bloody selfish!

[BEN *exits.*]

HENRY   I'm sorry.

A bright winter's morning.

HENRY   I couldn't face the thought of watching him leave. I said I had to go to the dentist and drove away without looking back. I had no idea where I was going. Then I realised it was the same road I'd taken with Joanna — that first day, when we went to Burford.

I stopped on the hill where we stopped in the summer. I played Ben Webster again. The countryside was very beautiful. A clear blue sky and, even at midday, a crisp carpet of frost.

I decided to drive to the hotel and have some lunch.

[BASSETT, *the hotel manager, enters.*]

BASSETT   Good morning, sir, can I help you?

HENRY   Good morning.

[BASSETT *looks at him. Pause.*]

BASSETT   What are you doing here?

HENRY   Lunch — do you have a table for lunch?

BASSETT   Please leave. I don't want you in this hotel.

HENRY   What ... ?

BASSETT   Leave the hotel, Mr Preece.

HENRY   What are you talking about?

BASSETT   Just do as you're told.

HENRY   I'm not doing any harm.

BASSETT   You wouldn't invite vandals into your house. I regard you as a vandal. You and people like you are destroying the moral values of this country.

HENRY   Don't be ridiculous!

BASSETT   Yes, I know common decency is despised these days, but I find it offensive that you should treat my hotel as a brothel.

[*He takes* HENRY *by the arm.*]

Come along.

HENRY   Don't do that.

BASSETT   Are you completely without any sense of shame? Have you never heard of self-denial?

[HENRY *is struggling to free himself.*]

HENRY   Let go! Let go of me!

[BASSETT *propels him towards the door.*]

BASSETT   I want you out of here!

HENRY   Take your hands off me! Let go!

BASSETT   Come along — *out!*

HENRY   How dare you!

[HENRY *punches* BASSETT *in the stomach. Taken by surprise,* BASSETT *gasps and staggers back.* HENRY *advances.*]

BASSETT   Don't do it — don't be foolish —

HENRY   How dare you treat me like this! — how dare you!

BASSETT   — I'm warning you —

[HENRY *goes to hit* BASSETT *again.* BASSETT, *an expert in unarmed combat, seizes* HENRY *and hurls him through part of the scenery.* HENRY *disappears from view. The broken section of scenery is replaced instantly.*]

[*The telephone rings.* KATE *enters and answers the call.*]

KATE   Hello?

BASSETT   Miss Preece?

KATE   Yes?

BASSETT   Good afternoon. My name's Bassett. I'm the manager of the Glebe Court Hotel in Burford.

KATE   Yes?

BASSETT   It's about your brother.

KATE   What about him?

BASSETT   There's been an accident —

KATE   Oh my God!

BASSETT   Nothing to worry about, no serious damage.

KATE   What's happened? Where is he?

BASSETT   We took him to Out-patients at the John Radcliffe Hospital. I'm afraid you'll have to collect him. He won't be able to drive.

KATE   Oh my God!

> [KATE *exits in a hurry.* BASSETT *exits.*]

Early evening. HENRY *is revealed, seated, heavily bandaged, with a plaster cast on his left arm.* POOLE *enters.*

POOLE   How are you feeling?

> [*No response.*]

Apparently he's the Karate and Kick-boxing Champion of Wiltshire. You weren't to know that, of course. [*sits down*] I understand completely why you were so angry. People with an unshakeable belief in their own point of view are always extremely irritating. Doubt is one of the least recognised of virtues. No one with any intelligence can be certain about anything — least of all morality. Do you mind if I smoke?

> [*No response.* POOLE *lights a cigarette.*]

In my view — it's all biological. Genetic. Everything goes back to primitive man, struggling for survival. Hundreds of thousands of years ago. The overriding concern was for the species itself: survival and propagation. What we now regard as sinful and immoral were, in fact, aspects of behaviour that could harm the development of the species. If we all told lies, the power of speech would become devalued and pointless — therefore, speak the truth. Sexual reproduction is good because the species is enriched by the genetic mixture of the two partners; sex between close relations is not so good; the genetic mixture is more restricted and thus of less value to the species — therefore, avoid incest. We're ruled by our genetic impulses. Certain acts are desirable, certain acts are to be deplored. God, The Great Disapprover, was invented much later. And along with God came heaven and hell, etcetera, guilt and shame, and so forth, which meant that morality and superstition became hopelessly confused. 'Commit adultery and you'll burn in hell forever.' Result: man lusting for his secretary takes a cold shower and goes home to his wife. He's not a moral man, just a frightened one. People avoid immorality for the same reason they avoid walking under a ladder: they're afraid something nasty's going to happen to them. Of course we all like to think that our actions are governed by something more substantial than primitive fears or irrational impulses — that's why we summon up a whole host of bogus authorities to give them the appearance of intellectual respectability: 'The Moral Values of Our Country' — 'What Decent People Think' — 'The Christian Way of Life' — these things don't really exist, they're just flim-flam: vague, woolly-minded clichés which we use to disguise the fact there are no moral facts, just feelings. That's why I gave up philosophy and became a policeman. I don't have to worry about what's right and what's wrong — the law does that for me. If I had to make any sort of moral judgement, I wouldn't know where to begin. [*rises to his feet*] What people lose sight of is the fact that our so-called moral rules aren't real rules — like in cricket or Monopoly. They're like trousers; they can be altered as we grow or change shape. We do our best to ignore that, because real rules are easier to handle; they can be blamed on somebody else: parents, God, the manufacturers of Monopoly. If it's just a matter of mutual agreement, mutual consent, then we've got no one to blame but ourselves.

Take your affair with Mrs Barley. I suspect that what really distresses you is not the fact of the affair, but the discovery that you were capable of it — and of all the concomitant lies, betrayals and deceit. That's the price you pay for taking moral choice into your own hands: large — and sometimes alarming — revelations of self-knowledge. A door has been opened: perhaps you wish it had been left closed. [*stubs out his cigarette*] Your son telephoned, by the way. Checking to see if there was any news of his mother. I didn't tell him about the fracas at the Glebe Court Hotel. [*goes to the door*] Mr Bassett has decided not to bring charges against you. But you'll have to pay for all damage to hotel property. Fair enough?

[POOLE *exits. Lights fade on* HENRY.]

Day. ALEXANDER *enters*.

ALEXANDER We were driving along the M11 towards Cambridge. Jo was sitting beside me; she had sunk into a deep depression. She hadn't spoken for half an hour. I thought to myself, if I drive fast into the crash-barrier we'll both be killed and all this misery will be over. I imagined the moment when the metal would slice into us. Blood gushing onto the windscreen. Jo screaming. For a moment, my foot actually pressed down on the accelerator. Then I saw a sign saying Exit 9. That was the exit I wanted. Obediently I slowed down and drove onto the slip road and thence towards Newmarket and Thetford. Jo's depression lifted. We stopped at a Little Chef for a cup of coffee. A child at the next table squirted tomato ketchup over his sister's ice-cream. Everybody laughed. We drove on. Jo played a cassette she'd just bought. Ben Webster. Marvellous.

[ALEXANDER *exits*.]

HENRY, *with all his bandages removed, enters and sits at the table.* JOANNA *enters and goes to him. They greet each other with a kiss on the cheek.* JOANNA *sits down. A* WAITER *serves.*

HENRY   It's good to see you.

JOANNA   And you.

HENRY   How are things?

JOANNA   Fine.

HENRY   Alexander ... ?

JOANNA   Yes, he's fine.

HENRY   Does he know we're having lunch?

JOANNA   Yes, of course.

HENRY   Doesn't he mind?

JOANNA   Why should he?

[*Pause. They eat.*]

HENRY   It seems very distant.

JOANNA   Does it?

HENRY   Us, I mean.

JOANNA   I know what you mean.

HENRY   Don't you think?

JOANNA   Sometimes.

HENRY   Sometimes I can't believe it ever happened.

JOANNA   Sometimes it seems very close.

HENRY   Yes.

[*Pause. They eat.*]

JOANNA   We're moving.

HENRY   What? Where?

JOANNA   Norfolk. Alexander's been offered a good job. Better school.

HENRY   When?

JOANNA   Soon. He'll start at the beginning of next term.

HENRY   Do you want to move?

JOANNA   I don't mind. Norfolk's nice. We can go sailing.

HENRY   I didn't know you liked sailing.

JOANNA   Didn't you?

> [*Pause.*]

HENRY   I'm glad Alexander's all right. I didn't want to mess up his life.

JOANNA   You didn't.

HENRY   Nearly.

JOANNA   It wasn't your fault.

HENRY   It all began when I asked you out to lunch.

JOANNA   It would've happened anyway.

HENRY   Would it?

JOANNA   Oh yes. Things were bad between me and Alexander.

HENRY   But they're better now?

JOANNA   Better. Yes. Better.

> [*Pause. They eat.*]

No news of Angela?

HENRY   No.

JOANNA   Do you miss her very much?

HENRY   Sometimes. It varies. Sometimes I can hardly remember her; at other times I can't believe she's not going to come barging into the kitchen laden with Sainsbury's carrier bags.

> [*Pause. They eat.*]

JOANNA   What happened about the book? Did you finish it?

HENRY   No.

JOANNA   You should. It's good.

HENRY   It's pointless.

JOANNA   It's not.

HENRY   Totally pointless.

JOANNA You only think that because you're depressed.

[*No response from* HENRY.]

Did Ben read it?

HENRY He's not interested in that sort of thing.

JOANNA Did you show it to him?

HENRY No.

[*He sips his wine.*]

JOANNA I saw my sister last week. We talked about you. 'How's that man you used to work for?' she said. She knew nothing about — what happened.

I suppose I thought my life would be like hers. Children, an Aga, a Volvo estate.

I never expected to marry Alexander. We went to bed together because I had a crush on him. It never occurred to me that we might be found out.

[*She raises her head and looks at* HENRY.]

It was different with you. I fell in love with you.

[HENRY *looks at her. She stretches out her hand towards him. He does not reciprocate. She withdraws her hand.*]

Perhaps I'd better go. I mustn't be too late.

[*She rises to her feet and looks down at* HENRY.]

I'm sorry.

HENRY For what?

JOANNA If it hadn't been for me, this would never have happened.

HENRY Don't be ridiculous.

JOANNA It's true.

HENRY I don't know what you mean.

JOANNA I wanted us to make love. I set out to make it happen. Deliberately.

[HENRY *stares at her.*]

You've got nothing to feel guilty about.

> [HENRY *gives a bark of mirthless laughter.*]

Nothing. She found out. She ran away. All because of me.

HENRY   That's just nonsense.

JOANNA   It's not your fault, Henry.

HENRY   You don't understand. I killed her.

> [JOANNA *stares at him.*]

JOANNA   What?

> [*Pause.*]

HENRY   It was about five past ten. Just after I rang the police. I heard a noise in the hall. I went out and there she was. 'Where have you been?' I said, 'I've just rung the police.' 'Yes, I know,' she said, 'I heard.' She walked past me into the sitting room. She was smiling. 'Have you had a nice day?' she said. 'I suppose you've been with your mistress.' I just stared at her. I didn't know what to say. She kept on talking. She kept calling you my 'mistress'. 'How is your mistress?' 'Is she a good fuck?' She started making jokes — saying she was surprised I could remember how to do it. Then she sat down and pretended to watch television, just to annoy me. I picked up the heavy glass ashtray and hit her hard across the side of the head. By the temple. She fell forward. I hit her again. I got a sheet and wrapped her in it. I carried her to the bottom of the garden. I'd been clearing bracken and undergrowth. I hid her there. Then the policeman came. A young police constable. He told me not to worry. I got up early the following morning. I burned her with the flame-gun we got from the hire shop in Cirencester. I dug a deep trench. I put her in it. I covered her with leaves and undergrowth. I burned everything with the flame-gun.

[JOANNA *stands very still, looking at him.*]

JOANNA Oh God. Oh God. Oh God.

[JOANNA *runs out.* HENRY *cradles his head in his hands. He weeps.*]

KATE *enters.*

KATE Henry didn't want to stay with me and he didn't want to go back to Stoke Amberley, so he moved into a motel on the M4. Strange, really, since he hates motorways. After a month or so, he decided to put the house on the market and move back to London. He found a flat near the Finchley Road.

I was glad to see him go. As much as I love him, I realised I was also bored by him. I was bored by his obsessive punctuality and his obsessive tidiness. I found him difficult to live with. He's also an obsessive checker. He checks everything at least twice. Some evenings I thought I'd scream as I saw him checking the gas taps before we went to bed. Perhaps that's why Angela left him. Perhaps she got bored as well.

[KATE *exits.*]

Evening. Deep shadows. HENRY *is wrapping cups and saucers in newspaper and stacking them in a tea-chest. A second, full, tea-chest stands nearby.* ALEXANDER *enters.*

ALEXANDER Hello, Henry. How are you?

[HENRY *looks at him but says nothing.*]

I've come to say goodbye. We'll be leaving on Thursday. I gather you're going too.

[HENRY *nods.*]

How are you feeling?

HENRY All right.

ALEXANDER   Tell me the truth.

[HENRY *does not respond.*]

You must be feeling very low.

[HENRY *does not respond.*]

Perhaps I could help.

HENRY   I can't see how.

ALEXANDER   Maybe I can.

[*He goes to* HENRY *and sits by him.*]

When I was a boy, I wanted to be a priest. I believed I had a real vocation for the church. But as I grew older, I turned away from God. It wasn't until I thought I'd lost Jo for ever that I began to pray again. I begged God to forgive me. My prayers were answered. Jo was returned to me.

[HENRY *remains motionless and silent.*]

She told me what you said. About Angela. She knows it's not true. She knows you made it up. She doesn't understand why. I do. I understand completely.

[*He takes* HENRY *by the hand.*]

God cares for us all and loves us. Ask Him to help you and to forgive you. Ask for His blessing, Henry. His mercy is infinite.

[HENRY *looks at him. He withdraws his hand from* ALEXANDER'*s gentle grasp. Pause.*]

HENRY   You see, the point is, I think we've got it all wrong. People assume that humankind must be the crowning glory of creation. That's just nonsense. We're the results of over-ambition. It's like a carpenter who's wonderful at making chests of drawers trying his hand at the Eiffel Tower or a Boeing 747. Of course he fails miserably and quickly resumes the mainstream of his work, i.e. chests of drawers. God over-reached himself with man. Where he succeeded admirably was with trees. Look at them. Perfect. I imagine God sitting in a shady bower of oaks and sycamores and copper beech, waiting patiently for man to destroy himself, which, no doubt, he will do very shortly. We're just a faux pas. A blot. A discard. An error of judgement. Why should anyone care about us?

[ALEXANDER *is silent for a moment.*]

ALEXANDER   In many ways, I blame myself. I should've realised there was something going on. I mean, looking back — it seems so obvious. I must've been blind or stupid. Or both.

[*He expects some response from* HENRY *but there is none. He gives him a change of address card.*]

Well, anyway — here's our new address. Do keep in touch.

[HENRY *takes the card.*]

HENRY   Thanks.

ALEXANDER   Good luck.

HENRY   And you.

[ALEXANDER *exits.*]

A bright sunny day. POOLE *enters.*

POOLE   A friend of mine in Bournemouth sent me a cutting from his local newspaper. Apparently Henry Preece had gone there to visit his former partner (now retired), Graham Walker. He'd been shopping in the local supermarket. On his way back to his car, he seemed to see someone he recognised driving out of the car park. Passers-by said he dropped his shopping bags and ran headlong after a departing car. He was shouting something, but nobody could quite understand what it was.

HENRY   Angela! — wait! Angela!

POOLE He wasn't looking where he was going. A delivery lorry was approaching in the opposite direction. There was no way the driver could stop in time. Henry died in the ambulance, on his way to hospital. I have heard no more of Mrs Preece. Had there been a gruesome discovery, no doubt it would have made the headlines. So one must assume that she is alive and well, living a new life in what one hopes is quiet contentment. But of course that sort of news never makes the front page.

THE END